The Seventeenth-Century English Hymn

American University Studies

Series XX
Fine Arts

Vol. 5

PETER LANG
New York • Bern • Frankfurt am Main • Paris

Thelma B. Thompson

The Seventeenth-Century English Hymn

A Mode for Sacred and Secular Concerns

PETER LANG
New York • Bern • Frankfurt am Main • Paris

Library of Congress Cataloging-in-Publication Data

Thompson, Thelma B.
    The seventeenth-century English hymn : a mode for
sacred and secular concerns / Thelma B. Thompson.
        p. cm. — (American university studies. Series XX,
Fine arts ; vol. 5)
        Bibliography: p.
        Includes index.
        1. Hymns, English—History and criticism.
2. English literature—Early modern, 1500-1700—History
and criticism.   I. Title.   II. Series.
BV312.T45   1989   264'.094209032—dc20   89-7995
ISBN 0-8204-0695-3   CIP
ISSN 0890-412X

CIP-Titelaufnahme der Deutschen Bibliothek

Thompson, Thelma B.:
The seventeenth-century English hymn : a mode
for sacred and secular concerns / Thelma B.
Thompson. — New York; Bern; Frankfurt am
Main: Paris: Lang, 1989.
    (American University Studies: Ser. 20,
    Fine Arts; Vol. 5)
    ISBN 0-8204-0695-3

NE: American University Studies / 20

© Peter Lang Publishing, Inc., New York 1989

Printed by Weihert-Druck GmbH, Darmstadt, West Germany

For my parents and all others
who taught me to love hymns
and to practise the Golden Rule
and, also, for Lisa

ACKNOWLEDGEMENTS

I am deeply grateful to my mentor, Dr. Ivan Taylor, Professor Emeritus, Howard University, for his guidance and assistance with this work. Dr. Estelle Taylor, Former Chairperson of the Department of English, Howard University offered me much advice for which the manuscript is better. I thank Dean Evans Crawford and Professors Charles Walker Thomas of Howard University and Dr. Esther Ward of Bowie State College for their advice also.

Finally, I thank my family as well as special friends for their support and understanding and Mrs. Carole DaCosta for her undying patience with the preparation of the typescript.

Thelma B. Thompson
1989

ACKNOWLEDGMENTS

TABLE OF CONTENTS

INTRODUCTION

One of the literary contributions of seventeenth century England to western civilization is the English hymn. Having its birth in the political and religious turmoil of the age, the seventeenth-century hymn bears the marks of its genesis from the church, the court, and the schools. Not surprising is the fact that the general body of seventeenth century English literature shared these same origins. The hymn is herein treated as lyric poetry and the definition embraces the seventeenth century poems that were adapted for congregational singing, although most of these older hymns often contain strong elements of history, philosophy, politics, metaphysics or a combination of these elements.

The religious battle for the legalization of hymn-singing was won during the earlier years of the seventeenth century and the hymn itself was used as a weapon in this fight. Related to this function of the seventeenth century English hymn is its overwhelming use by various religious and political bodies to disseminate their doctrines and convictions. In addition, this study revealed a type of hymn that could bed termed "counter-doctrinal," a type of hymn which does not support a particular doctrine but, rather, refutes logically one or several doctrines.

Serving as a mode through which the religious rights of a person could be asserted, the seventeenth-century English hymn was used, at times, as a mode of expressing the spiritual autobiography of its author. This vehicle of expression is evident in a hymn such as John Bunyan's "To be a Pilgrim."

Often the hymns revealed conflict between the old religious beliefs such as Apostolic Succession and more modern seventeenth-century concepts such as Divine Right of Kings. One result of such conflict was the posture of wavering and of vacillation in hymn writers such as George Wither.

Beyond the above application, the seventeenth-century hymn served as a medium for the spiritual and political education of the masses. Since many churchgoers then were not formally educated, the hymn writer simplified doctrinal tenets and rendered them comprehensive and memorable to laymen. Although dogmatic and didactic, the English hymn of the seventeenth century bears striking similarity to the general body of seventeenth-century literature; for themes such as the schism in the Church remained the subject of many poems and prose works during that age.

Since no clear lines of demarcation exist between the politics and the religion of the seventeenth century, it seems accurate to describe some seventeenth-century hymns as political. Such hymns seem to provide a safe stance from which the hymn writers could attack political opponents or defend their own postures. This research shows that such hymns were possibly the forerunners of the body of English hymns classified as nationalistic, militaristic, or warlike.

Additionally, this research reveals that even hymns of praise
and contentment, at times, originated from the fragile and
tenuous security of seventeenth-century English political life.
This study covers the period from the death of Queen Elizabeth
I to the close of the reign of Queen Anne (1603-1714). Mention
is made, however, of the hymn writers of other countries and
centuries for the sake of comparison, or to demonstrate a
particular strain or influence.

Graphically evidenced in the seventeenth-century English
hymn is the transition from the medieval, theological, and
deductive to seventeenth-century, logical, and inductive belief
and thought. Numerous scientific developments such as the
heliocentric theory, physics, astronomy, mathematics,
chemistry, geography and map making, new food substances, new
philosophical theories such as neoplatonism, and social
developments such as institutionalized slavery all found
expressions in the English hymn. On the other hand, frequent
mention of witchcraft, evil spirits, devils, magic and alchemy
is made in these hymns. These beliefs sometimes persisted even
in hymns in which newer beliefs appear. These hymns,
therefore, reflect not only the transitional nature of the
seventeenth-century but also, over-whelming concern with
secular matters.

This work posits, finally, that the seventeenth-century
English hymn should be regarded as a genre in itself. Because

4

of the diversity of its sources and the emphasis that has been placed on the mode for its religious and utilitarian values, no clearly definable school of writers of the seventeenth-century English hymn was emerged. Seventeenth-century literature, nevertheless, took as its subject matter both sacred and secular concerns and rendered these concerns in forms that are still popular today. From this vantage point, these hymns are transcripts from life holding their historical as well as their artistic integrity and demonstrating that they form a mode for expressing the sacred and secular concerns of their age.

SUMMARY OF HISTORICAL EVENTS AFFECTING THE
DEVELOPMENT OF THE SEVENTEENTH CENTURY ENGLISH HYMN[1]

1530 and 1540   The Reformation of the Church - 16th Century
Miles Coverdale published <u>Goostly Psalms</u> and
<u>Spiritualle Songes</u>.

1559   The Injunctions of Queen Elizabeth--gave free
permission to use "any hymn or such-like song
in the praise of almighty God at the beginning
and end of morning and evening prayer."

1603-25   JAMES I. Puritan clergy ask freedom in
ritualistic details: James orders them to
conform or leave the ministry. Puritans left
the country.

1611   King James Version of the Bible.

1625-49   CHARLES I. Religious differences: Archbishop
Laud represses Puritans and Presbyterians.

1637-38   Troubles with Scottish Covenanters;
Presbyterianism established.

1642-47   Civil War: Col. Cromwell develops cavalry
regiment of Puritans; Struggle for power
between Presbyterians and Separatists

---

[1]The information for these charts came mostly from the following sources: Louis F. Benson, <u>The English Hymn</u>; John Julian, <u>Dictionary of Hymnology</u>; Albert E. Bailey, <u>Gospel in Song</u>; Henry Smith, <u>Lyric Religion</u>, Sir Paul Harvey, <u>The Oxford Companion to English Literature</u> and my general knowledge.

	(Independents). Cromwell favored the latter.
1643	Westminster Assembly
1645	Archbishop Laud executed; victory of Presbyterians and Independents over Anglicans.
1649	Charles I executed. England declared to be a COMMONWEALTH, without king or House of Lords. Oliver Cromwell Protector.
1653	Cromwell and army ejected Presbyterians from Parliament and made Independents supreme. Cromwell made Lord Protector.
1654	Puritan religion established, supported by tithes. Ministers were any brand of Puritanism (neither Anglican nor Catholic).
1658	Cromwell died: Richard Cromwell, his son, succeeded.
1660-85	CHARLES II. The Restoration (1660).
1661	Corporation Act: Office-holders must take Sacrament administered by Anglican Church (Non-conformists thus excluded from Parliament).
1661	Savoy Conference: to review for Charles II, The Book of Common Prayer.
1662	Act of Uniformity: Clergyman and schoolmasters refusing to consent to everything in the Prayer Book, excluded from holding a benefice.

Two thousand clergy resigned. (Henceforth,
all who refused to assent were called
Dissenters.)

1664   Conventicle Act: Any person attending a
Dissenting meeting was punished with up to
seven years' "transportation" deportation.

1665   Five Mile Act: Dissenting ministers never to
come within five miles of former preaching-
places.

1673   Test Act: Office-holders must swear disbelief
in Catholic doctrine of Transubstantiation,
and receive Sacrament by Anglican clergymen
(Catholics thus driven from office; Dissenters
usually conformed.)

1685-89 JAMES II (a Roman Catholic)

1686   Judge Jeffries persecutes Dissenters but
favors Roman Catholics.

1687   James issues Declaration of Indulgence,
suspending all laws against Catholics and
Dissenters. Anglican clergy resist. Seven
bishops jailed but acquitted.

1688   James II issued the Declaration of Indulgence,
and seven bishops among them, Bishop Ken, were
committed to the Tower of London. People
were aroused by their danger. Starting on the

west coast, they marched to London singing:

> "And shall Trelaway die, and
>   must Trelaway die?
> Then twenty thousand Cornish men shall
>   know the reason why
> And shall the bishops die, And must the
>   bishops die?
> Then one hundred thousand Englishmen
>   shall know the reason why."

1689-1702 WILLIAM AND MARY. Parliament declared for Protestant succession hereafter. <u>Toleration Act</u> (1689) gave Dissenters (except Unitarians and Catholics) right to worship publicly and freely.

1702-14 QUEEN ANNE: Strong for Anglican Church and Tories. Rise of Deism: (Reason the sole test of religion) God revealed in a world of law.

1703 New version of Tate and Brady Psalter with hymns authorized for use in the Church by Queen and Council, July 30.

1711 Jonathan Swift uses satire against Whigs, Catholics, and Dissenters. Occasional Conformity Act: Penalized dissenters who received Anglican Sacrament to get office, but continued to attend Dissenting Churches.

1714 Schism Act: No one could keep a school without a license from Anglican bishop.

1714-27 GEORGE I: Favorable to Whigs, Dissenters, and traders. Much political corruption: Tories stood for religious intolerance and contempt for trade; Whigs for toleration and weakening power of king. Both used bribery.

DEFINITION OF TERMS RELEVANT TO THE STUDY OF
THE SEVENTEENTH CENTURY ENGLISH HYMN

<u>Catholic:</u> Literally, the word means universal and is applied
to various sects that claim a world-wide authority. (Cf. the
phase in the Apostles' Creed in the Anglican Prayer Book: "I
believe in the Holy Catholic Church.") Ordinarily, the term is
limited to the Roman Church, the government of which is
exercised by authority from the top (from the Pope),--through
cardinals, archbishops, bishops, priests--rather than by
authority from the bottom, as in democratic Congregational or
Baptist Churches. Its theology is that of Thomas Aquinas,
thirteenth century. In this paper, Catholic refers to the
latter definition.

<u>Protestant:</u> One who protests against the authority or the
belief of the Roman Catholic Church. The term covers all of
the Churches which are mentioned below:

<u>Anglican:</u> The word is the same as "English" when
applied to religious matters. The Anglican Church is
the "Established" English Church which began its
independent existence when Parliament proclaimed
Henry VIII to be the head of the Church in England
and declared the Church's independence of Rome. The
term covers all Churches that hold the same faith
(beliefs), order (government by bishops, priests and
deacons), and worship (the use of the Prayer Book),--

mostly in the British Empire. The Episcopal Church in America is essentially, though not technically Anglican.

Established Church: One supported by the civil authority and paid for out of taxation.

Puritan: One who opposed the traditional forms of faith, order, and worship of the Anglican Church and strove for "purer" or simpler forms. For example, Puritans objected to prescribed cross in baptism and to the theatre. They felt that authority should come from the people rather than from the bishops and clergy. At first, the Puritans did not advocate withdrawal from the Established Church.

Puritans became strong in the reigns of Elizabeth I and James I, and were the dominant political party in the days of the Commonwealth. The term came to cover several varieties, namely:

Independents (Separatists, Congregationalists): Puritans who separated themselves from the Established Church and set up their own organizations on a democratic, self-governing basis. In theology they were Calvinistic. They were severely persecuted under Elizabeth I and James I. Many fled to Holland and later to America, twenty thousand of them by 1640.

Presbyterians: A form of independent Church in which the government is by presbyters or elders, elected

by the members of individual church bodies; and the whole
collection of churches is regulated by a system of courts
made up of ministers and elders. These courts are called
Synods, Sessions, General Assemblies; in theology, the
Presbyterians are Calvinists. (The Scottish Church was
Established Presbyterian until 1929, when it ceased to be
established but remained Presbyterian.)

Baptists: Churches that are congregational in
government, mostly Calvinistic in theology, and insist
that church membership is open only to adult believers who
have been baptized by immersion, as opposed to baptism of
infants and baptism by sprinkling or pouring. They were
an offshoot of an old continental sect--the Anabaptists.
The first English Baptist Church dates 1611. There are
various brands.

Non-Conformists: This new term arose in 1662 to cover anyone
who refused to conform to the ritual and discipline of the
Established Church. Primarily, it applied to the two thousand
clergymen who would not submit to the Act of Uniformity of 1662
and so were put out of their churches. The Act required that
everything contained in the Book of Common Prayer--be carried
out exactly.

Dissenters: One who dissented from the doctrines of the
Established Church; the term is used loosely a synonym for Non-
conformists; though strictly speaking, non-conformity has to do

with acts, while dissent has to do with belief.

<u>Non-Juror:</u> The beneficed clergy who in 1689 refused to take the oath of allegiance to William and Mary.

CHAPTER I

THE HYMN AS LITERATURE

In England the seventeenth century was an age of change
and transition. This fact may be observed in the literature,
in general, and in the English hymn, specifically. As it is
known today, the English hymn was forged in the controversial
fires of the seventeenth century. This is not to suggest that
the hymn was born then, for some of the medieval hymns of
England still stand to testify to the fact that hymnody was a
part of the religious life of medieval worship. Rather, the
seventeenth-century hymn marks the resurgence of hymnody,
through this revival, the hymn became typically English, that
is to say, hymns became a mode for free religious and musical
expression distinctly different from the metrical settings of
the Psalms. Prior to that age, hymn writing was limited to
religious scholars and inspired men.

It is a befitting circumstance that one of the earliest
literary pieces extant in English literature is Caedmon's
"Hymn," a fragment, yet an authentic song in praise of the
Creator. Caedmon, who lived around 670 A.D., is often regarded
as "The Father of English Song."[1] Born of divine inspiration,
Caedmon's hymn is unlike the modern hymn, yet this fragment
conforms to St. Augustine's definition of a hymn, one of the
oldest definitions which states:

> It [a hymn] is the singing to the praise
> of God.
> If you praise God and do not sing, you utter no
> hymn.
> If you sing and praise no God, you utter no hymn.
> If you praise anything which does not pertain to the
> praise of God, though in singing, you praise, you
> utter no hymn.[2]

Hymn writing flourished in the great monastic centers of medieval learning, and although these hymns were composed in Latin, one must bear in mind that at the time Latin was not a dead language. Instead, in the Christianizing of England, Latin played an important role. Latin was, according to Albert C. Baugh, "the language of the services and of ecclesiastical learning . . . and some of their scholars . . . were versed in the Greek and Latin tongues as in their own, in which they were born."[3]

It is important to note that there are in popular use today hymns that were composed by medieval hymn writers. In fact, Charles S. Nutter thinks that the hymn "Jerusalem the Golden," written by Bernard of Cluny in the twelfth century, may be "pronounced the most beautiful of all medieval hymns," and he agrees that "the heavenly heartache, with the soul enamored of its home in the skies and longing to depart, never ... found a sweeter or more touching expression than in these hymns of Bernard."[4]

From this discussion, it appears that Carl Price is correct in stating that the development of the hymn has the shape of the hourglass. It has a broad base in Greek and Latin hymnody, it tapers around the time of St. Augustine, and then it expands "through wider usage to our modern idea of a hymn."[5] It is the second surging of the hymn that will be of major concern, herein.

The hymns of the seventeenth century formed the foundation of the modern English hymn and reflect the political and religious turmoil of a nation in transition. Indeed, political concerns of that age were generally, also, religious concerns because the king was involved in matters of Church as well as in matters of state. Hymns arose out of the factionalism and competitions of the times, and the English hymn of that era sets the direction for later hymn writers.

The students of hymnology will learn very early of the great contribution that Isaac Watts made to hymnology, but they will learn also to examine Watts in proper perspective. As Louis Benson explains, "between the Restoration and the Revolution there arose a considerable group of original hymn writers, whose work in volume, in character and influence, counted for something in the history of the English hymn. These early writers deprive Dr. Watts of that extreme originality often ascribed him as 'The Father of the English Hymn'"[6] This "something" of which Benson speaks is the courageous and continuous effort that these early hymn writers put forth as they sought means for free and creative expression.

Up to the present, there has been much written about Greek, Latin, and Medieval hymns. There are several notable works, such as John Julian's <u>Dictionary of Hymnology</u>, Louis Benson's <u>The English Hymn: Its Development and Use</u>, and Benjamin Brawley's <u>The History of the English Hymn</u>, which cover the development and history of the hymn. Critical studies, however, have been confined to the individual works of hymn writers. With the exception of works about Bunyan, the studies are confined to Isaac Watts and later hymn writers. Little critical study has been made of the seventeenth-century hymn as literature of its age. This study will attempt to relate the seventeenth century English hymn to its contemporary literary works and to consider the hymn as direct expressions from its authors.

One of the major concerns of those interested in such a study as this is to arrive at an acceptable definition of the term "hymn" as attempts have been made at such a definition. For example, Lord Selbourne in the Preface of <u>The Book of Praise</u> gives this definition:

> A good hymn should have simplicity, freshness, and reality of feeling; a consistent elevation of tone, and a rhythm easy and harmonious, but not jingling or trivial. Its language may be homely but not trivial or mean. Affectation or visible artifice is worse than an excess of homeliness. A hymn is easily spoilt by a single falsetto note. Nor will the most exemplary soundness of doctrine atone for doggerel, or redeem from failure a prosaic, didactic style.

Whereas St. Augustine is concerned with the purpose of
the hymn, Lord Selbourne is more concerned with its total
structure, substance and tone. He is also mindful of its
spiritual impact, and this latter description is one step
closer to the real anatomy of the hymn. Yet, it is important
to note that sound doctrine is an expected component of a good
hymn as Selbourne conceived it. Carl Price agrees with Lord
Selbourne that a hymn must be poetic in form as well as
substance. He insists that a hymn must be lyrical not only in
its relationship to music, but also in tone.[8] It seems, then,
that man's hymn is a prayer and that as a prayer, it cannot be
called simply a devotional lyric or a song of praise, for man's
prayer voices the wide range of his needs, his disaffections,
his sorrows, and his aspirations. It seems, consequently, that
two definitions already published best answer the question
"What is a hymn?" Generally, Dr. Benjamin Brawley accepted the
definition of a hymn as "a religious ode or poem; . . . a
metrical composition divided into stanzas or verses, intended
to be used in worship."[9] More specifically, the definition set
forth by the Hymn Society of America best defines the hymn as a
modern genre as well as a genre from its inception. The
definition states:

> A Christian hymn is a lyric poem,
> reverently and devotionally conceived,
> which is designed to be sung and which
> expresses the worshipper's attitude
> toward God, or God's purposes in human

> life. It should be simple in style,
> spiritual in quality, and in its ideas so
> direct and so immediately apparent as to
> unify a congregation while singing it.[18]

Since the main characteristics of the hymn are "lyric" and

"poem," and these characteristics must be included in any

discussion of the seventeenth-century hymn, it seems logical

and appropriate to adopt this comprehensive definition as a

basis for this study that treats the English hymn as

literature.

Over the years, some literary critics have excluded the

hymn from the realm of literature mainly because the hymn is

sung in a religious context and is "a blend of facts, symbols,

persons and other nameless qualities."[11] Certain qualities in

a hymn, however, are beyond the critics' analytical dissection

because the whole hymn possesses emotive qualities that the

individual parts of that hymn do not have. The uniqueness of

the hymn should enhance its status, but this quality has not

been the basis of evaluation of this genre.

To poets such as Milton and Spenser, the term hymn meant

religious ode. Thus, in "The Hymn" of "On the Morning of

Christ's Nativity," Milton sings praise to the peace that the

Christ child brings to the world. As is the case with several

hymns composed during the seventeenth century, this hymn was

not meant for congregational singing; however, many such hymns

have survived because they have been adapted to hymnody.

Students of hymnology are in general agreement that the

hymn is a lyrical poem, a status that unquestionably places it
in the realm of literature. Jeremiah B. Reeves complains of
the treatment given the hymn:

> The hymn as the most ancient type of
> literature and as a most pervasive and
> powerful kind of poetry has not had its
> dues from critics. They have not so much
> frowned upon the hymn as they have given
> it a sort of differential toleration,
> exempting it from liabilities as well as
> its rights in the realm of letters.[12]

Reeves is quite accurate in his accusation. Hymns have been of
interest historically, but for themselves, they have not been
explored as the rich domain of poetry which the constitute.

Perhaps the question of the status of the hymn has its
roots in a basic belief of Isaac Watts that the hymn "must be
kept outside the realm of poetry--stripped of poetic
suggestiveness and be written down to the level of the meanest
capacity."[13] Yet, Watt's theory should not be wholly accepted
as an accurate description of his own practice or that of his
fellow hymn writers. On the contrary, it can be demonstrated
that the criterion of John Wesley and not Watts is more
accurate in representing the actual status of the hymn. Louis
Benson states Wesley's criteria for the hymn as follows:

> The work of the Wesleys set up a new
> standard in Hymnody on its literary side.
> Their hymns are in line with the earlier
> devotional poets rather than with Watts.
> They controvert Watts's canon of hymn
> writing and laid down a new one,--a hymn
> should be a poem . . . Wesley maintained
> that the Hymn should be a religious lyric
> and create the impression of lyrical

22

poetry; that masses must be lifted up to
the level of the Hymn and made to feel
the beauty, the inspiration of poetry.[14]

John Welsey's criterion was prescriptive, but an actual

examination of the use of hymns, from the seventeenth century

on, will demonstrate that it is also descriptive. Furthermore,

Wesley repeatedly used verses from the poetry of George Herbert

in his own hymns, and Herbert's poetry is among the most

intellectual and poetic of the seventeenth century. In some

cases, John Wesley adapted several of Herbert's poems in their

entirety and rearranged them for congregational singing by

altering their metre. The following example of Wesley's

adaptation of Herbert's poem "The Dawning" shows how easily the

change was made:

> Awake sad heart, whom sorrow ever drowns!
> Take up thine eyes which feed on earth.
> Unfold thy forehead gather'd into frowns.
> Thy Savior comes, and with him mirth,
>   Awake, awake!
> And with a thankful heart his comforts take.
> But thou dost still lament, and pine, and crie,
> And feel his death, but not his victorie.
> Arise sad heart! If thou dost not withstand,
> Christ's resurrection thine may be,
> Do not by hanging down break from the hand
> Which as it riseth, raiseth thee.
>   Arise, arise!
> And with his buriall-linen drie thine eyes.
> Christ left his grave-clothes that we might,
>   when we grief
> Draw tears or bloud, not want an hand
>   kerchief.[15]

John Wesley's adaptation of this hymn appears in the

following form in his _Hymn and Sacred Poems_ of 1739:

> Awake sad Heart, whom sorrows drown

Lift up thine eyes and cease to mourn,
Unfold thy Foreheads settled frown
Thy savior and they Joys return.

Awake, sad drooping Heart awake!
No more lament, and pine, and cry;
His Death Thou ever dost partake
Partake and last his Victory

Arise, if thou dost not withstand,
Christ's Resurrection Thine may be;
O break not from the Gracious Hand
Which as it rises, raises thee.

Chear'd by thy Saviour's Sorrows rise,
He griev'd That Thou mayst cease to grieve;
Dry with his Burial Clothes thine Eyes
He dy'd Himself that thou mayst live!

The changes that Wesley makes in this adaptation are minor. He reduces the stanza to four lines and partially regularizes the meter. Wesley adheres closely to Herbert's ideas, but in Stanza I, he simplifies the thought. Line two in Herbert's poem reads, "Take up thine eyes, which feed on earth." This line suggests the sinner's posture of down-cast eyes and sadness. It also hints that earthly things do not inspire the heart, and further, that the earth is man's end. On the other hand, Wesley's line reads, "Lift up thine Eyes, and cease to mourn," thereby weakening the rich association of ideas in Herbert's lines. The cause for sorrow is not included in Wesley's version; the sinner is merely commanded to lift up his eyes and to cease to mourn as though there were no logical connection between the two. In Stanza II, Wesley omits Herbert's idea of the thankful heart. This is a serious deletion because Herbert used opposites for emphasis: instead

24

of being sorrowful, the Christian ought to be thankful and

accept Christ's "comforts." Herbert's argument again attempts

to supply some reason for the recommended action, but Wesley's

does not.

Herbert's hymn was included in the <u>Moravian Collection of</u>

<u>Hymns</u> of 1754 in the following form:

> Awake sad heart, whom sorrow drowns
> Unfold thy forehead from its frowns,
> Take up thine eyes which feed on earth
> Thy savior comes and with him mirth!
> He left his Grave-cloaths that we might
>   when grief
> Draws sighs and tears, not want a Handkerchief.
>
> Now, heart! if thou dost not withstand,
> Nor handing down, break from his Hand,
> Christ's Resurrection thine may be;
> He as he riseth raiseth thee,
> That as his Death had calcin'd thee to dust,
> His life may make thee Gould and much more
>   just.[16]

A closer adherence to Herbert's original hymn is noticeable in

the version included in the <u>Moravian Collection.</u> The lines are

as irregular as Herbert's and the hymn is not stripped of its

rich associations. This and several others of Herbert's hymns

such as "Throw away Thy Rod" and "My stock lies dead and no

increase" have been omitted from the more modern editions of

the <u>Moravian Collection</u> and the <u>Wesley Hymn Book</u>, but others

remain in common use and will be examined later in this book.

It must be borne in mind that although a large percentage

of the seventeenth-century congregation was illiterate, their

hymn writers were not. Many hymn singers then as now, may not

have been able to analyze the poetic techniques involved in the
construction of a hymn, but what is more important is that they
understand its meanings. It is frequently the case,
furthermore, that the only poetry with which the unlearned man
comes in contact is the hymn, and it is often the only poetry
which he voluntarily memorizes and regularly uses. Despite the
success, popularity, and universality of the hymn, it is
usually excluded from anthologies of poetry and it is generally
ignored by teachers of poetry. A small body of hymns, however,
forms an exception of this practice. These hymns have long
been recognized for their splendid poetic qualities. For
instance, "The spacious firmament on high" by Joseph Addison is
studied as an expression of deism; hence, this hymn is famous
for its philosophical ideas proclaiming the power of the
Creator of the universe. Also, "The Olney Hymns" of William
Cowper and John Newton enjoy popularity as examples of the pre-
romantic gloom in poetry. Cardinal John Henry Newman's "Lead
kindly light" is important as a testimony of the spiritual
development of its author. Finally, Rudyard Kipling's
"Recessional" represents, among other things, the historical
and patriotic stance of England during the nineteenth century
as well as a warning against pomp and vain glory.

These hymns and others help to exemplify the real nature
of the English hymn that is marked by its variety and
versatility. In addition, the English hymn contains

philosophy, or history, or politics, or metaphysics, or a
combination of these elements. Hymns, moreover, often indicate
autobiographical data such as the conversion of their writers,
as in the case of Newton and Newman. Additionally, the hymn is
artistic in its structure, often using the infinity of space
and time to create metaphorical comparisons and, thus, inspire
its singer. The seventeenth-century hymn is the archetype of
the English hymn and as such contains most, if not all, the
features observable in later hymns.

Caroline Whitemarsh and Anne Guild, in describing the
source of the hymn, claim that it emerges from the same sources
as other great writings:

> [from] the whole vast range of Christian
> thought, experience and imagination . . .
> from among the lofty strains of Ambrose
> and Jerome . . . from the secret cells
> and the high cathedrals of continental
> worship, where scholarship, and art and
> power joined with piety to raise Lauds
> and Glories . . . from the purer
> literature of Old England, embracing the
> tender numbers of Southwell, and Crashaw
> and Habington.[17]

Commenting on the hymn as poetry, William G. Horder makes a
necessary distinction by pointing out that although these early
hymns voiced prayer, praise, confession, or communion, they all
had poetic unity, and the poetic unity rendered all hymns
sacred poems, but not all sacred poems hymns.[18]

It is the same idea of unity in a hymn that Frederick
Saunders believes to be its highest literary merit:

> Hymns are not meant to be theological
> statements . . . they are utterances of
> the soul in the manifold moods of hope
> and fear, joy and sorrow, love, wonder
> and aspiration. A hymn should not
> consist of comments on a text or of
> remarks on an experience, but of a
> central and creative thought, shaping for
> itself melodious utterance and with every
> detail subordinated to its clear
> harmonious presentation. Herein a true
> hymn takes rank as a poem.[19]

Frederick Gillman contradicts Saunders and best describes the total literary validity of the English hymn. His statement applies particularly to the seventeenth-century English hymn, for according to him these, more than any others, arose out of the circumstances of their age. Gillman, thus, makes the following observation concerning the literary significance of the hymn:

> To get behind the hymnbook to the men and
> women who wrote its contents, and to the
> events, whether personal or public, out
> of which it sprang and which it so
> graciously mirrors, is to enter into a
> world palpitating with human interest.
> For a hymn book is a transcript from real
> life, a poetical accompaniment to real
> events and real experiences. Like all
> literature that counts, it rises directly
> out of life . . . The heart of the
> Christian church is revealed in its
> hymns; and if we take the trouble to
> relate them to the circumstances that
> gave birth to them, we shall find they
> light up with fresh meaning.[20]

Although Gillman and Saunders complement each other, it seems logical to observe that each one is correct in part. A hymn which is merely a "theological statement," "a transcript

of life," or a "comment on a text" will not achieve its purpose
as a hymn. They agree, nevertheless, that a hymn should be an
utterance of the soul, rising directly out of the experiences
of life. It is possible, indeed, for an idea based on
theology, or on an experience, such as the hymn, "Lead kindly
light," to begin as such, and later to transcend the bonds of
the specific and the actual circumstance and to achieve a high
level of "creative" and spiritual thought. This possibility,
then, makes the hymnbook more than a "transcript from real
life."

The historical approach to the hymn which Gillman
advocates is necessary, for no other approach adequately places
the seventeenth-century hymn in its true perspective. For
example, in the light of what Gillman says, a hymn by George
Herbert states clearly what a hymn should achieve: an accord
between the human soul and the lines of the hymn, and a
stirring of the heart as well:

A TRUE HYMNE

> My joy, My life, My crown!
> My heart was meaning all the day,
> Somewhat it fain would say;
> And still it runneth mutt'ring up and down,
> With only this, My Joy, My Life, My Crown!
>
> Yet slight not these few words;
> If truly said, they may take part
> Among the best in art.
> The finenesse which a hymne or psalme affords
> Is, when the soul unto the lines accords.
>
> And all the soul, and strength, and time,
> If the words onely rhyme,

Justly complains that somewhat is behinde
To make his verse, or write a hymne in kinde.

Whereas, if th' heart be moved,
Although the verbe be somewhat scant
God doth supplie the want.
As when th' heart sayes (singing to be approved)
Oh, could I love! and stops. God writeth, Loved.[21]

Herbert's title is somewhat ambiguous; he is describing the
true hymn, not offering this selection as an example of one.
Cecil Northcott points out that hymns classified as "Chiefly
Devotional" are sometimes not singable, but only readable. Yet
he thinks that these devotional poems may be called hymns since
they answer to the canons laid down by Isaac Watts, that "they
should express thought and feelings."[22] Thus Herbert's "Hymne"
sheds light on his theory of a true hymn and exemplifies the
scant "verbe" in fine metaphysical irregularity. This thought
of Herbert's is one upon which evaluation of the hymn as a
literary subject has rested. For many, the conventional,
mechanical, stanzaic form precedes the hymns, and may suppress
the innate organic form of some hymns, thus retarding the
development of their fullness from within. Although in the
final stanza, Herbert's "Hymne" deals with a metaphysical
concept of God's understanding of man's insufficiency, he uses
that idea merely as a comparison for supporting this theory of
hymn writing. In Stanza I, the speaker, though desiring to
write, finds himself at a loss for words. Yet, he, like Sir
Philip Sidney, the Elizabethan lyricist, realizes that if the
words can be so arranged that they appeal to the hearts of

men, then a greater artistic purpose is served. In short,
Herbert is advocating content over form, or thought over
structure for excellence in hymn writing. This concern has
remained a vital one for poets of all ages.

James Montgomery joins the group of hymnologists who
believe that the hymn is poetic not only in form, but also in
structure, yielding greater appreciation with each repetition.
He states:

> A hymn ought to be regular in its
> structure as any other poem; it should
> have a distinct subject, and that subject
> should be simple, not complicated, so
> that whatever skill or labor might be
> required in the author to develope his
> plan, there should be non required on the
> aprt of the reader to understand it.
> Consequently . . . there should be a
> manifest gradation in the thoughts and
> their mutual dependence should be so
> perceptible, that they could not be
> transposed without injuring the unity of
> the piece . . . . Transcendently
> superior in value as well as influence,
> are those hymns, which, once heard, are
> remembered without effort . . . with
> renewed and increasing delight.[23]

English hymns, then, establish themselves as poetry
although the cannon is varied in texture. For example, Felix
Schelling thinks that William Cowper's "Olney Hymns" need not
be read, since they represent inferior lyrics.[24] Like the
quality in any other body of literature, the quality of
seventeenth-century hymns is uneven. Benjamin Brawley states
that although their moods express powerful feelings, some of
the best-known and best-loved hymns have literary faults.[25]

Benson echoes Brawley, and in his discussion of the hymn not merely as literature, but as the literature of power, says, "It [the literature of power, the hymn] will sometimes preach, while it pretends to sing, and even tread on a critical canon or two as it hews its way to men's hearts."[26] Nancy Thomas also points out that "whether the hymn be good poetry or bad poetry, good music or bad music, it is poetry and music. It is simply not possible to disrobe the religious message of its garments . . . and have much of vital significance left. The three--religious idea, poetry, and music--are a unity . . . as far as full meaning is concerned.[27] Indeed, as Jeremiah Reeves observes, "hymnody constitutes a part, not only of English literature, but of all literature. Historically, the human race was up and singing before sunrise."[28] Indeed, the hymn, like other lyrical poetry, may be narrative or expressive, conversational or devotional. It makes use of the persona, points of view, rhythm, rhyme, tone mood, theme(s), and more than any other type of poetry, strives for clarity and appropriateness in diction. Several hymns in use today have survived for three or four centuries and from the positions they hold in hymnody will survive for many generations to come. In short, these hymns are classical literature and should be accorded some degree of appreciation.

To ignore the hymns because of any short-comings they might display is to diminish the literary legacy of western civilization. Writings, especially the earliest forms in a genre, mark the beginnings of that genre and have much to teach. Any later advancements, developments, and improvements in thought or techniques relate directly to the earlier starting point. The seventeenth century English hymns mark such beginning and they carry the scars and shields to testify to their honored position in English literary history.

NOTES FOR CHAPTER I

[1]Louise Pound, "Caedmon's Dream Song," <u>Studies in English Philology</u> (1929), p. 232.

[2]Carl F. Price, "What Is a Hymn?" <u>Papers of the Hymn Society of America</u>, No. 6 (1937), p. 3.

[3]Albert C. Baugh, <u>A History of the English Language,</u> 2nd ed. (New Jersey: Prentice Hall, 1957), pp. 96-97.

[4]Charles S. Nutter and W. F. Tillett, <u>The Hymns and Hymn Writers of the Church</u> (New York: Eaton and Mains, 1911), pp. 320-321.

[5]Carl F. Price, "What Is A Hymn?", p. 3.

[6]Louis Benson, <u>The English Hymn</u>, reprint (Richmond, Virginia: John Knox Press, 1962), pp. 71-72.

[7]W. Garrett Horder, <u>The Hymn Lover</u> (London: J. Curwen and Sons, c. 1889), pp. vii-viii.

[8]Price, "What Is A Hymn? p. 5.

[9]Benjamin Brawley, <u>History of the English Hymn</u> (New York: The Abingdom Press, 1932), p. 13.

[10]Price, "What Is A Hymn?" p. 8.

[11]Caroline Whitemarsh and Anne Guild, compilers, <u>Hymns of the Ages</u> (Boston: James R. Osgood and Co., 1877), p. viii.

[12]Jeremiah B. Reeves, <u>The Hymn as Literature</u> (New York and London: The Century Co., 1924), n.p.

[13]Benson, <u>The English Hymn</u>, p. 252.

[14]Benson, pp. 252-253.

[15]George Herbert, <u>The English Works of George Herbert: Vol. III, Bemerton Poems</u>, George Herbert Palmer, arranger (Boston: Houghton and Mifflin Co., 1905), p. 333.

[16]Moravian Church, <u>A Collection of Hymns of the Children of God in All Ages from the Beginning till Now</u> (London, 1754), Part I, 360.

34

34

[17]Whitemarsh and Guild, p. ix.

[18]William Garret Horder, The Hymn Lover, p. viii.

[19]Frederick Saunders, Evenings with the Sacred Poets (New York: T. Whittaker, 1899), p. 272.

[20]Frederick J. Gillman, The Evolution of the English Hymn (New York: The Macmillan Co., 1927), p. 30.

[21]Bourchier Saville, comp. Lyra Sacra: A Collection of Hymns Ancient and Modern (London: Longman, Green, London and Roberts, 1861), p. 135.

[22]Cecil Northcott, Hymns in Christian Worship: The Use of Hymns in the Life of the Church (Richmond, Virginia: John Knox Press, 1964), p. 2.

[23]James Montgomery, The Christian Palmist or Hymns (Glasgow: William Collins, c. (1825) pp. xiv-xvi.

[24]Felix E. Schelling, The English Lyric (Boston and New York: Riverside Press, Houghton and Mifflin, 1913), p. 139.

[25]Brawley, History of the English Hymn, p. 11.

[26]Benson, The English Hymn, p. vi.

[27]Nancy Thomas, "The Philosophy of the Hymn," Papers of the Hymn Society No. xxi (New York: Hymn Society of America, 1956).

[28]Reeves, The Hymn as Literature, pp. 13-14.

CHAPTER II

HISTORICAL BACKGROUND OF THE SEVENTEENTH-CENTURY
ENGLISH HYMN

The year 1603 marks, in English history the end of Queen
Elizabeth's long reign (1558-1603). Since the Queen had left
no natural heir, the accession of James I of England (James the
Sixth of Scotland, 1567-1603) resulted in unrest and
dissatisfaction. Because James I was the son of Mary Queen of
Scots,[1] (Mary Stuart, a Roman Catholic, and cousin to Elizabeth
I of England), he was not fully welcomed as king. To aggravate
the political situation, James I introduced two doctrines which
intensified the strife. The first, the policy of High Church,
forced the Church of England to stress the sacerdotal,
liturgical, and traditional ceremonial Roman Catholic elements
of worship. The emphasis on ceremonial, outward display of
pomp, appeal to the senses, as evidenced in clerical vestments
of elaborate design, genuflections and the use of candles,
crosses, stained-glass windows, paintings, music, and statues
for symbolic, decorative purposes was especially offensive to
the Puritans who considered such practices as relics of popery
with no authority in the word of God.

Even more offensive to the Puritans was King James I's
doctrine of the Divine Right of Kings. The Puritans were
seeking to simplify church doctrines, to bring the common man
in closer contact with the spiritual life of the church, and

to have church government organized from the congregation upward rather than from the archbishop downward. Both these doctrines were in direct opposition to the Puritans' objectives; hence, in 1603, one thousand clergymen petitioned the king, and the king ruled that the clergymen must conform to both the doctrines of the Divine Right of Kings and of High Church or leave the ministry.[2] As a result of this act, thousands of Puritans sailed to Holland and America, but thousands of determined men and women, nevertheless, remained to fight for their beliefs.

The bitter struggle continued through the reign of Charles I (who held his father's beliefs) and its culmination was the Civil War of 1642-1646. In the midst of this controversy, the English hymn flourished and, for the first time, it became a vehicle for expressing much of the dissatisfaction with the times. This aspect of the seventeenth-century hymn will be discussed fully in a later chapter. However, it must be remembered that among the many issues over which disputes developed, the Bible, the Prayer Book and the Psalter were prominent. In these times, moreover, it is important to remember that a man's religion was often dictated by his political affiliation and that there was no distinct demarcation between Church and State. For example, in 1559, the Injunctions of Queen Elizabeth gave free permission for the use of "any hymn or such-like song in the praise of Almighty

God at the beginning and end of morning and evening prayer,"[3]
and an entry in the revision made of the Book of Common Prayer
by the Savoy Conference of 1661 shows that there must have been
singing in some churches. Among the changes that were made is
the addition of "five prayers (including the state prayers
which had previously been appended to the Litany) to the Divine
Service." The rubric concerning these prayers for Mattens and
Evensong mentions an anthem "in quires and places where they
sing."[4] This anthem is not mentioned in the earlier Prayer
Books, but there is other proof that hymns were allowed in
Anglican churches prior to 1660.

A study of the rubric of various editions of the Book of
Common Prayer yields the following: "The Liturgy of the
Ancients" instructs, after the communion: "then this Hymn," and
"Glory be to God on High." is printed as the hymn. Also,
Bishop Laud's Prayer Book of 1637 shows some vacillation. In
"The Order of the Administration of The Lord's Supper or Holy
Communion," the following direction is given after "The
Thanksgiving:" "Then shall be said or sung, Gloria in Excelsis
in English." Finally, in the text of the liturgy written by
Bishop Jeremy Taylor, the directions after communion read as
follows: "Then shall follow this Eucharistical Hymn, all
standing up reciting the verses interchangeably." Especially,
the Injunction of Queen Elizabeth in 1559, gave permission for
the singing of hymns in the following clause:

> For the comforting of such as delight in
> music, it may be permitted that in the
> beginning or end of Common Prayer, either
> morning or evening there may be sung an hymn
> or such-like song to the praise of Almighty
> God in the best melody and music that may be
> devised, having respect that the sentence of
> the hymn may be understood and perceived.[5]

The Queen's order authorizes and encourages singing so that the

"sentence," the meaning of that unit of thought, will be

perceived. This latter requirement is a distinct break with

psalm-singing wherein the phrasing was dictated by the music

and not by the meaning of the sentences.

It appears that some efforts were made to follow the

Queen's recommendation. Speaking of the seventeenth century

The Oxford History of Music reports:

> The attitude of the composers was not
> devotional. They did not include beauty or
> any appeal to the softer sentiments as things
> worth trying for. The main difference
> between the new sacred and secular music was
> no more than in degree of seriousness for
> they paid strict attention to word.[6]

In addition, the old version of the English Psalter of 1561

which contains several hymns has the following long title:

"The whole Booke of Psalmes, collected into Englysh metre by T.

Starnhold, I. Hopkins & others conferred with the Ebrue, with

apt notes to sing them withal, Faithfully perused and allowed

according to thordre appointed in the Queens maiesties

Iniunctions. Very mete to be used of all sortes of people

priuately for their solace and comfort: laying apart all

vngodly Songes and Ballades, which tende only to the nourishing of vyce, and currupting of youth".

Because the word "privately" is used in this title, and because that word remained in the title of the Psalter until 1566, Louis Benson claims that the hymns appended to the English Psalters from 1561-1635 do not form the nucleus of English Hymnody. Benson comes to the following conclusion:

> It is then obvious that the presence of these hymns in the English Psalter does not of itself imply, either in intention or fact, their use in the church services. As to the actual significance of their inclusion one must form his own conclusion.[7]

According to the dates on the Psalters, the word "privately" remained in the title for only five years. One may suggest that five years is not an extended period and, further, that its removal after so brief a stay may very well suggest that the practice of using these hymns publicly may have made the change urgent. Beyond this projection, there are three observations which tend to support the postulation that these, or other hymns, were used.

First, there is internal evidence in one early hymn that leaves the implication that it may have been used at Holy Communion. The hymn written by Thomas Campion (1567-1620) follows:

> View me, Lord, a work of thine:
> Shall I then lie drowned in night?
> Might thy grace in me but shine,
> I should seem made all of light.
>
> Cleanse me, Lord, that I may kneel
> At thine altar, pure and white:

They that once thy mercies feel
Gaze no more on earth's delight.

Worldly joys, like shadows, fade
When the heavenly light appears;
But the covenants thou hast made,
Endless know nor days nor years.

In thy word, Lord, is my trust;
To thy mercies fast I fly;
Though I am but clay and dust,
Yet thy grace can lift me high.[8]

The hymn writer is asking to be cleansed so that he may kneel
at God's altar, "pure and white." In Anglican Liturgies, a
prayer for the cleansing of communicants has always held its
position before the sacrament of Holy Communion is offered.
This hymn would have been an appropriate one at such a time.

Secondly, in the limited canon of seventeenth-century
hymns, an unusually high proportion of morning and evening
hymns appears. It is understood that in the regular Christian
household in seventeenth-century England, devotions were held
morning and evening and probably many of these hymns wre
written with that in mind. Also, in the case of Bishop Ken, he
wrote for the daily devotion of his school boys as well as
himself. Yet these hymns found their way into the early
hymnbooks because they became the business of demand and supply
was as much a factor as the preference for hymns over psalms.
Many of these hymns were written by Elizabethan writers such
as Gascoigne, Thomas Browne, and Edmund Spenser who, generally,
lived in the earlier years of the century or in the latter part
of the preceding century. Several examples which will best

portray the idea exist and appear in Table I.

TABLE I

Examples of Seventeenth-Century Evening Hymns

"When thou hast spent the ling'ring day," George Goscoigne (1525-1527), The Clarendon Hymn Book, No. 30.

"The night is come like to the day," Thomas Browne (1605-1682), The Clarendon Hymn Book, No. 29.

"Christ who knows all his sheep," Richard Baxter (1615-1691), The Clarendon Hymn Book, No. 143.

"Behold the sun that seemed but now," George Wither (1588-1667), Oxford Hymn Book, No. 18.

"Glory to thee who safe has kept," Thomas Ken (1637-1711), Oxford Hymn Book, No. 1.

"Glory to thee in light arrayed," Thomas Ken (1673-1711), Oxford Hymn Book, No. 16.

"Awake my soul and with the sun," Thomas Ken (1673-1711), Hymns Ancient and Modern, No. 3.

"All praise to thee, my God, this night," Thomas Ken (1673-1711), Hymnal of the Episcopal Church, No. 18.

"Most glorious Lord of life that on this day," "Edmund Spenser (1552-1599), The Clarendon Hymn Book, No. 34.

"Hail thee! Festival day," Edmund Spenser (1552-1599), The Clarendon Hymn Book, No. 101.

It seems that the relatively large number of morning and evening hymns exists because hymns for those occasions were particularly authorized by the Queen's injunction.

Finally, John Austin's hymn, called "Sunday," quoted below, offers internal evidence of singing in the last verse.

> Behold we come, dear Lord, to thee,
> And bow before thy throne;

We come to offer an our knee
Our vows to thee alone.

Whate'er we have whate'er we are,
Thy bounty freely gave;
Thou dost us here in mercy spare,
And wilt hereafter save.

Come then, my soul, bring all thy powers,
And grieve thou has no more;
Bring every day thy choicest hours,
And they great God adore.

But, more than all, prepare thine heart
On this, his own blest day,
In its sweet task to bear they part,
And sing, and love, and pray.[9]

Austin's hymn seems to be designed for public use because the two opening stanzas are in the plural. It suggests Christian fellowship. The final stanza reinforces that suggestion, for people do, in fact, assemble to "sing, and love, and pray."

Finally, the edition of the Prayer Book which resulted from the Savoy Conference (1661) instructs that the creed "may be said or sung" after the Epistle. In "The Ordinal" of that edition, Bishop Cosin's translation of the Veni Creator, "Come Holy Ghost our Souls Inspire" as well as "Christ our Passover" and the "Gloria" were added along with several Easter Anthems.

It appears that the changes in The Book of Common Prayer were related to the political climate of the seventeenth century. When Puritan power was at its highest, the directions for singing were either changed to "may be sung or said," or "to be recited," but when Puritan domination waned, singing became a natural part of the services. It is safe to conclude that if Puritan pressure groups had not agitated against hymn-singing, the Anglican Church would have been among the earliest bodies in England to promote singing, for the Sternhold and Hopkins Psalter of 1561 contained ten hymns, one of which is still in common use today:

> O Lord, turn not Thy Face from me,
> Who lie in woeful state.
> Lamenting all my sinful life
> Before Thy mercy-gate.
>
> A gate that opens wide to those
> That do lament their sin.
> Shut not that gate against me, Lord,
> But let me enter in.
>
> And call me not to strict account
> How I have sojourned here;
> For then my guilty conscience knows
> How vile I shall appear.
>
> Mercy, Good Lord, mercy I ask;
> This is my humble prayer;
> For mercy Lord is all my suit
> O let thy mercy spare.[10]

This hymn is written in the common meter of 8.6.8.6. with the a b c b ballad rhyme which was later popularized by Isaac Watts. It is clear and simple, ideal for unison singing.

Because of the effect of history upon the seventeenth-century hymn, critics tend to sum up the development of the hymns of that period in historical terms. For example, Mrs. Charles Rundel does so in these lines:

> In Church and State (1644-1700), every
> difference became a dispute; the electricity,
> which in calm weather, quickened life, and
> exploded into thunderstorms. Yet amidst the
> din, the old psalmody flowed on, piercing
> with its music all the clamor. George

> Herbert, ministering to the poor and borne
> to his grave with cathedral chants; blind
> Milton, Secretary of the Protector [Oliver
> Cromwell 1649-1658] and scorn of the court of
> the Restoration; Richard Baxter, true pastor
> of the flock of Christ, so basely brow-beaten
> by Judge Jeffreys; Bishop Ken, the non-juror-
> -these are the voices which carried on the
> song of peace through the time of strife.[11]

In this context, it is as though the hymn writers were inspired
to write and to express themselves in song, regardless of
political constraints. One may deduce that the hymns of the
age provided strength for the persecuted. Edward Bailey says
that the English Parliament could not "suppress the lyric soul
of England: it might forbid the use of hymns of human composure
. . . but it could not prevent a poet from writing or singing
in his own home, or in social gatherings."[12] Bailey observes,
further, that each hymn writer of the seventeenth century was
engaged in a struggle. The struggle was sometimes a personal
one, as Erick Routley points out. He says that although the
English hymn writers of the seventeenth century wrote of the
intimacies of faith, "the seventeenth century in its public
worship, was not an age of intimacy. It was an age of loyalty,
of controversy, of ferocity and bloodshed."[13] Horton Davies in
describing the developments in worship practices among
seventeenth century religious dissenters reminds readers that
the meetings of dissenters were illegal and so in Southwark,
dissenters refused to sing for fear of provoking a raid from
the authorities. But in Bristol, Dissenters sang loudly when

warned of raids to suggest to the policy that "innocent
singing" and not "illegal preaching was their only aim.[14]

Often, the controversy was over some practice of church
worship such as whether hymns could be sung in church. If they
could, then who should sing them, and who should compose them?
In fact, the Baptist Church split into hymn-singers and non-
hymn-singers during the seventeenth century.[15] The hymn-
singers sometimes used as their basis the fact that St. Paul's
advice to the Ephesians was to speak to themselves in "psalms,
and hymns and spiritual songs" (Ephesians 5:19). The Puritans
held the Bible to be the inspired word of God and the only
basis of truth. Consequently, they interpreted it literally.
This literal interpretation led to confusion, for one group
believed that only those hymns based on the psalms were
acceptable, while another group viewed such hymns as a
corruption of the psalms. Bishop Jeremy Taylor comments on the
situation of his time in these words:

> It is good that we transplant the instruments
> of fancy into religion, and for this reason,
> music was brought into the churches and
> comely garments and solemnities that the
> wandering eye and heart may be bribed and
> made so he be disposed to cherish a more
> spiritual affection.[16]

To the modern scholar, this comment could be captioned
"Non Puritan thought." It was made by one who was opposed to
Puritanism and who suffered at the hands of Puritans. The
scholar must question what reasons were there for factionalism,

for often the doctrines of sects seem quite similar except in minor matters of dress and music. A retrospective glance at the religious condition of the seventeenth century, the age in which freedom of worship was truly won at a high price, Ernest E. Ryden views the age as a typical one in history:

> It is hardly a coincidence that every great
> spiritual movement in the history of the
> church has been accompanied by a fresh
> outburst of song. It was so when Ephraim
> Syrus in the East, and St. Ambrose in the
> West tried to combat the Arian Heresy by
> teaching their followers to sing. It
> happened again when Luther seized upon this
> spiritual weapon in his heroic effort to
> cleanse the church of its errors and to lead
> men back to a saving faith in Christ.
> Again, it was so when the Wesleys sought to
> arouse their countrymen from spiritual
> indifference.[17]

This great interest in hymns in the seventeenth century started in hushed songs, for the congregations had to be taught how to sing. The metrical psalm, once the domain of priests and choristers, became the hymn of the ordinary man.

Presenting some difficulty to the unschooled congregation, the metrical psalm resulted in the lack of orderly singing and provided the basis for a quip from Shakespeare in his <u>Merry Wives of Windsor</u>:

> They do no more adhere and keep place
> together than the hundredth Psalm to the tune
> of Green sleeves.[18]

Routley provides the following explanation of this allusion:

> Sternhold . . . had written his psalms in
> ballad-metre presumably that they might be
> sung to some of the great old ballad tunes

under the general ascription of "English
Traditional Melody."[19]

Although the metrical psalms were dull and demanded strict

concentration on points and phrasing, the translated psalm

often was plain in meaning but coarse in language in its

attempt to render literal meaning. For example, Psalm XLII

begins as follows:

> As the hart panteth after the water brooks,
> So panteth my soul after Thee, O God.
> My soul thirsteth for God, for the living God:
> When shall I come and appear before God?

In contrast, the Sternhold and Hopkins Psalter of 1600 renders

this psalm thus:

> Like as the hart doth breathe and bray
> The well springs to obtain, so doth my soul
>   desire alway
> With thee, Lord, to remain.[20]

Admittedly, the psalter has simplified the psalm for the common

worshipper so that "panteth" becomes "breathe" and "bray."

These substitutions render the psalm immediately

comprehensible, but they diminish its diction and tone in the

process. Soon, however, the metrical psalmody widened to

accommodate songs, and a "native school of devotional poets

arose, who slowly discovered the distinction between a

meditative poem intended for private reading and edification

and a lyrical hymn to be sung in church."[21]

Benson points out clearly that the relatively late

development of the English hymn is due to the fact that the

English copied Calvin and became psalm singers, for the Psalms were closer to the Scriptures, while the Germans, under Luther,

because of their love of folk-songs, developed the hymn

somewhat earlier.[22] He states that the development of the hymn

from the metrical psalms proceeded along the following lines:

1. By way of an effort to improve the literary character
    of the authorized Psalter.
2. By way of an effort to accommodate the Scriptural text
    to the circumstances of present-day worship.
3. By extension of the principle of Scripture paraphrase
    to cover the evangelical hymns and other parts of the
    Bible.[23]

Benson's argument is acceptable, but the religious

controversies, it seems, stifled and retarded the development

of the English hymn; for although efforts were made towards the

writing of original hymns, social and political grievances

prevented their full flowering. John Julian summarizes the

situation thus:

> Lord Selbourne called Dr. Watts the father of
> English Hymnody: and, as having lifted
> English hymns out of obscurity into fame, the
> title is a just one. It will be seen,
> however, that there are facts in the history
> of the Metrical Psalters and obscure hymns
> which conditioned and moulded the work of
> Watts, that several of our choicest hymns in
> present use are found in books of the
> sixteenth and seventeenth century; that there
> are signs that hymns might have become a
> recognized part of church worship but for the
> Puritan reaction and that hymns, as distinct
> from paraphrases of Scripture, had become an
> acknowledged part of public worship among
> Baptists and Independents at the close of the
> seventeenth century.[24]

To Isaac Watts, however, goes the credit for unifying the

two strains of hymns-paraphrases of the Scriptures and

devotional lyric poetry. Watts also christianized the Psalms of David to render them more acceptable for singing.

It is necessary to mention one hymn writer at this point, whose efforts went partially to hymn writing and partially to fighting for the legitimacy of the hymn. Benjamin Keach, a Particular Baptist minister, and his congregation sang hymns distinctly from Psalms. First, he was converted to believe that "Congregational Song was an ordinance of Christ and undertook to realize his convictions among his own people. He obtained their consent to sing at the close of Lord's Supper about 1673 or 1675."[25] Later, Keach persuaded the congregation to consent to singing on Public Thanksgiving days, and then in 1790, on every Lord's day. Keach had to provide singing material, however, and he composed over three hundred hymns. The following hymn is a sample, representing a joyful, if not lyrical, mood, the stanzas weighted by worldly concerns:

A Mystical Hymn of Thanksgiving

My Soul mounts up with Eagles wings,
    And unto thee dear God she sings,
Since thou art on my side,
My Enemies are forc'd to fly,
As soon as they do thee espy;
    Thy name be glorify'd.

Thou makest rich by making Poor,
By Poverty add'st to my Store;
    Such Grace dost thou provide:
Thou would'st as well as thou mak'st whole,
And heal'st by wounding of the Soul,
    Thy name be glorify'd.

Thou mak'st men blind by giving sight,
And turn'st their darkness into light,

> These things cant be deny'd.
> Thou cloath'st the soul by making bare
> And giv'st in food when none is there;
> Thy name by glorify'd.[26]

The foregoing stanzas comprise only one-third of the entire thanksgiving hymn by Keach. The remaining six monotonous stanzas, continuing in the same manner, display the dichotomy of God's nature. Being generally repetitious, Keach's hymns do not progress.

Despite the fact that Keach wrote hundreds of hymns and may rightfully be honored as the father of Baptist hymnody, today's Baptist hymnals do not include Keach's efforts. Ironically, probably hinting at his own war with politicians, some of his hymns first appeared in 1676 under the title War With the Powers of Darkness. This Miltonic title offered a collection of dull, flat hymns, but these nonetheless, were the hymns that strove for and won legitimacy for the English hymn and so created the need for hymnbooks and that made the work of Watts and later hymn writers possible.

Although the Roman Catholic and Greek churches adopted singing of hymns as a vital part of their worship in the middle ages, this singing, like the reading of the Scriptures was most often done in an unknown tongue. James Montgomery observed in the introduction to the Christian Palmist that the use of unknown tongues was a display of craftiness by the learned who thought that "ignorance was the mother of devotion and the Ignorance [sic] was very willing to believe it."[27] One of the successes of the Reformation of the church was that psalms and hymns were revived and many were translated to the common tongue so that church people, learned and unlearned, could relate intellectually, spiritually, and emotionally to the texts that they sang. This feature is one that helped to account for the renaissance of the English hymn in the seventeenth century.

52

NOTES FOR CHAPTER II

[1]David Matthews, "James I of Great Britain," The New Encyclopedia Britannica (Chicago: Helen N. Benton, 1974).

[2]It has been of interest to may scholars to determine why James I was so inflexible. Of course, his mother was Catholic, but he was a Presbyterian and, therefore, should not have been so vehement in his injunctions. It seems that part of the explanation rests in the fact that James I became King of Scotland in 1567, when he was one year old. Consequently, all important decisions were made for him by Lords and Bishops. When James came to the English throne, he surrounded himself with similar advisers who stood to benefit from his decrees, and this fact led to his governing by proxy, leaving the kingly power in the hands of a few Bishops and noblemen and leaving the king free to establish his Catholic tendencies.

[3]Percy Dearmer, The Story of the Prayer Book in the Old and New World and Throughout the Anglican Church (London: Oxford University Press, 1933), p. 114.

[4]Dearmer, pp. 114-116.

[5]Julian, Dictionary of Hymnology, p. 917.

[6]The Oxford History of Music, Vol. III, The Music of the Seventeenth Century (New York: Cooper Square Publishers inc., 1973), pp. 281-282.

[7]Louis Benson, The English Hymn, p. 30.

[8]The Clarendon Hymn Book, No. 294.

[9]The Clarendon Hymn Book, No. 33.

[10]William H. Monk, compiler, Hymns Ancient and Modern (London: William Clowes and Sons, Ltd., 1815, 93.

[11]Henry Smith, Lyric Religion: The Romance of the Immortal Hymns (New York: The Century Co., 1931), p. 337.

[12]Edward Bailey, The Gospel in Hymns (New York: Charles Scribner's Sons, 1950), pp. 24-25.

[13]Erik Routley, "Muscular Christianity," Hymns and Human Life (Grand Rapids, Michigan: William P. Eerdman's Pub. Co., 1966), p. 53.

[14]Horton Davies, <u>Worship of the English Puritans</u>, (London: Dacrl Press, 1948), p. 171.

[15]John Julian, <u>Dictionary of Hymnology</u> (London: John Murray, 1925), p. 349.

[16]Saunders, <u>Evenings with the Sacred Poets</u>, p. 252/

[17]Ernest E. Ryden, <u>The Story of Christian Hymnody</u> (Rock Island, Illinois: Augusta Press, 1959), p. vii.

[18]William Shakespeare, <u>The Merry Wives of Windsor</u>, The Pelican Edition (Baltimore: Penguin Books, 1963), II.i. 56-57.

[19]Routley, <u>Hymns and Human Life</u>, p. 53.

[20]Samuel Duffield, <u>English Hymns: Their Authors and History</u> (London and New York: Funk and Wagnalls, 1884), p. 42.

[21]Frederick J. Gillman, <u>The Evolution of the English Hymn,</u> p. 155.

[22]Benson, <u>The English Hymn</u>, p. 20.

[23]Benson, p. 46.

[24]Julian, <u>Dictionary of Hymnology</u>, p. 343.

[25]Benson, <u>The English Hymn</u>, pp. 97-100.

[26]Benjamin Keach, <u>War With the Devil</u>, or <u>The Young Man's Conflict with the Powers of Darkness</u> (London: Printed for Benjamin Harris, 1675), pp. 116-117.

[27]James Montgomery, <u>The Christian Palmist</u> (Glasgow: William Collins c. 1825) introduction.

CHAPTER III

RELIGIOUS DOCTRINES IN THE SEVENTEENTH-CENTURY ENGLISH HYMN

The seventeenth-century English hymn is unique in the respect that the historical echoes of the Reformation of the church are chronicled in some of these hymns. They are poems written without the distance of a narrator, or without a definite assumed point of view. The poets, it was understood, expressed their own ideas when they wrote and they had to bear the consequences of their expressed thoughts. These were the times when favor with the courts meant goodwill or ill will. These were the days when within the recent memory of the English, monarchs were put to death and celebration of The Mass was a capital offense.

The English hymn of the seventeenth century became a medium through which several poets of that age expressed their religious beliefs and doctrines. Among these doctrines are those of Catholicism as well as Calvinism which includes predestination, election and perseverance of the saints, punishment for personal sin and original sin, the depravity of man, the authority of the Bible, and ancillary tenets of moderation and self-denial.

Michael Walzer points out that Calvinism is based on the premise that man is out of favor with God because of Adam's sin,[1] a premise that allows the acceptance of the doctrines of original sin and the depravity of man. These doctrines appear

in the seventeenth-century hymn, particularly in the hymns of
Isaac Watts. The third stanza of the hymn "Eternal Spirit we
confess" illustrates these doctrines in part.

> They power and glory work within
> And break the chains of reigning sin;
> Our wild, imperious lusts subdue
> And form our wretched hearts anew.[2]

While mentioning the "chains of reigning sin," this stanza
functions in two senses. First, it bespeaks the legacy of sin
passed down in man's very nature from Adam to all men.
According to the Calvinist doctrine, this "chain" can be broken
only by God's grace. In Calvinism, sin is frequently thought
of as bondage, or a heavy yoke that chains man to his baser
parts. The hymns of Isaac Watts abound with references to man
as a fallen creature[3] and to Adam as the cause of original sin.
For example, these stanzas show the acceptance of that theory:

> Oh! how shall fallen man
> Be just before his God?
> If he contend in righteousness,
> We fall beneath his rod.
>
> . . . .
>
> Ah! how shall guilty man
> Contend with such a God?
> None, none can meet him, and escape,
> But through the savior's blood.[4]

And again, in yet another hymn, Watts promotes the doctrine of
original sin:

> Adam our father and our head,
> Transgressed and justice doomed us dead
> The fiery law speaks all despair
> There's no reprieve, no pardon there.

> Lord, I am vile, conceived in sin,
> And born unholy and unclean,
> Sprung from the man whose guilty fall
> Corrupts his race and taints us all.[5]

So bluntly expressed are the ideas that the didactic purpose of these hymns becomes obvious. It appears also that Isaac Watts inspired, wrote partially as a validation of his faith and also as he was inspired by the various Psalms. Many of his hymns are based explicitly on specific Psalms. Unlike Isaac Watts, John Donne wrote his "Hymn to God the Father" for personal meditation. Yet, this hymn clearly expresses a belief in the concept of original sin:

> Wilt thou forgive that sin where I begun,
> Which is my sin, though it was were done before?
> Wilt thou forgive that sin through which I run,
> And do run still, though still I do deplore
> When thou hast done, Thou hast not done,
> For I have more.
>
> Wilt thou forgive that sin which I have won
> Others to sin? and made my sin their door?
> Wilt thou forgive that sin which I did shun
> A year, or two, but wallowed in a score?
> When thou hast done, Thou hast not done
> For I have more.
>
> I have a sin of fear, that when I have spun
> My last thread, I shall perish on the shore;
> But swear by Thyself, that at my death Thy Son
> Shall shine as He shines now, and heretofore
> And having done that, thou hast done,
> I fear no more.[6]

Donne's bent for punning in no sense diminishes the Calvinistic concepts of original sin and personal sin, for what the poet states is that having forgiven his sins, God is not done with Donne who will continue to sin. This hymn was set to music and

sung during John Donne's deanship at St. Paul's Cathedral.[7]
Its modern version, moreover, is like the original, except that
the first two lines read: "Will Thou forgive that sin by man
begun/Which was my sin though it were done before?[8] The
change from "where I begun" to "by man begun" is an effort to
make the hymn more universal in its appeal and less of a
private devotional one. The change, however, does not achieve
fully this intent because the rest of the hymn remains in the
first person and restricts the hymn to the original use, a
personal one. The second change is merely one of tense.
"Which is my sin," becomes "which was my sin," a change that
destroys the sense of the stanza, for the hymn seeks an answer
to the question, Wilt Thou forgive? When read in the past
tense, the question becomes redundant for since the sin "was,"
then there is now no need to ask forgiveness. Furthermore, the
rest of the hymn remains in the present tense, rendering the
single change in tense ineffective.

Holding more than semantic interest, this hymn by Donne is
asking a most serious question, and his concern in this hymn is
with original sin as well as man's personal sin. The form of
the hymn enhances the meaning and together they fuse in a
vibrant, poetic unity. Donne asks if God will forgive the sin
which is his although the sin were "done before." This is
original sin transmitted through his father "Donne" before him,
thus, punning on his family name here. Then Donne explains

that even if God were to forgive him his original sin, he would still "have more" sin, his personal sin.

In opening the second stanza with the question, "Wilt thou forgive that sin which I have won/Others to sin and made my sin their door," Donne shows that his personal sin leads others to original sin for the reason that children born to him have made his "sin their door." This line touches one of the most controversial questions in the concept of original sin, and great debates of the seventeenth-century churchmen argued the position of infants and children with respect to sin. However, Donne does not attempt to query the matter. He tells God that even when He has forgiven the original, the personal, and the offsprings' sins, He still has not completed His task, and by extension of the pun, He still will not "have Donne." It is only when God forgives his sin of fear and doubt that He will have done, that is to say He will possess Donne and be done with the work of forgiveness. The hymn demonstrates Donne's concern with sin. In this respect, his hymn is a doctrinaire as Watts's although it is far more metaphysical and witty.

Cheerful and light-hearted in its celebration of the extinction of original sin, Henry Vaughan's "Easter Hymn" represents an opposing view. The hymn appeared, originally, in his collection of poems Silex Scintillans in the following form:

       Death and darkness get you packing,
       Nothing now to man is lacking;

60

> All your triumphs now are ended
> And what Adam marr'd is mended;
> Graves are beds now for the weary,
> Death a nap to wake more merry,
> Youth now, full of pious duty,
> Seeks in thee for perfect beauty,
> The weak and aged, tir'd with length
> Of daies, from thee look for new strength;
> And infants with thy pangs contest
> As pleasant, as if with the breast.
> Then, unto Him, who thus hath thrown
> Even to contempt thy kingdome down;
> And by his blood did us advance
> Unto his own Inheritance,
> To Him be glory, power, praise,
> From this, unto the last of daies.[9]

This hymn appears in the <u>Clarendon Hymn Book</u> (no. 90) with no changes in the words except modernization of the spelling. It is, however, divided into three stanzas, the first two with four lines each and the last with six. The title is simply "Easter."

Because it demonstrates what could be termed the "counterdoctrinal" hymn, a term meaning that it does not strongly support a particular doctrine but, instead, refutes a doctrine in a logical manner, the hymn is of great importance to this argument. Vaughan's hymn refutes the doctrine of original sin on several points. Since man can seek his own redemption, then he establishes the position that the gloominess of death is no longer necessary. Additionally, death can no longer triumph over life; because atonement for Adam's sin is complete. The weary, weak, and aged can now die in peace, for there is assurance that the blood of Christ has advanced man to the status of Child of God. Finally, infants can now be as comfortable in the pangs of death as they would be at their mothers' breasts. The doctrine of original sin which held that infants born of non-elected parents were lost, and that infants born of elected parents were also lost souls if they died prior to their baptism, is a radical refutation of this doctrine of atonement. Easter is, therefore, a celebration honoring Christ whose death destroyed the "kingdom" of death and darkness and, in essence, set man free to seek redemption or "his own inheritance." The title of the hymn "Easter" becomes important in this instance because the focus is upon the death of death itself and not solely upon the resurrection of Jesus. The striking language of Donne and Vaughan as is demonstrated in these hymns contribute to the polysemus effect of the seventeenth century English hymn. Using the closed couplet, the hymn writer refines such a hymn so that it carries appeal even to simple folk who may not be able to fathom the metaphysical ideas that form the framework of the hymn. Sufficient at such a level, is the lively tone of the hymn set by use of slang such as "get you packing," to indicate the spirit of joy. Sufficient also are the homely images of napping and the infant snuggled at its mother's breast to evoke the feeling of trust and comfort. Hymns such as these are most successful in a literary sense because the diction, the structure, the tone and the theme combine to produce an effective whole, greater than any one of its parts.

The following hymn by Isaac Watts summarizes the seventeenth-century Puritan attitude toward the belief in man's depravity. He entitled it "Original Sin" or "The First and Second Adam":

> Backward, with humble shame we look
> On our original,
> How is our nature dashed and broke
> In our first father's fall!
>
> To all that's good, averse and blind,
> But prone to all that's ill;
> What dreadful darkness veils our mind!
> How obstinate our will!
>
> Conceiv'd in sin, (oh wretched state!)
> Before we draw our breath
> The first young pulse begins to beat
> Iniquity and death.
>
> How strong in our degen'rate blood,
> The old corruption reigns,
> And, mingling with the crooked flood,
> Wanders through all our veins!
>
> Wild and unwholesome as the root
> Will all the branches be,
> How can we hope for living fruit
> From such a deadly tree?
>
> What mortal power from things unclean
> Can pure productions bring?
> Who can command a vital stream
> From an infected spring?
>
> Yet mighty God, thy wondrous love
> Can make our nature clean,
> While Christ and grace prevail above
> The tempter death and sin.[10]

In this hymn, no recognition is given to man's better nature. Man is totally vile and lost. The diction abounds with harsh negative words such as "backward," "shame," "dashed," "broke," "fall," "averse," "blind," "darkness," "obstinate," "iniquity,"

"corruption," "crooked," "unwholesome," "deadly," and
"infected," a combination of negatives suggesting man's
powerlessness to save himself. Man's only hope of redemption,
therefore, rests in God's love and His grace, for according to
Calvinist theology, grace is a supernatural gift to which man
has a right. It raises them above the level of their nature
and permits them to see God face to face at the end . . . . We
have a right to it.[11]

Although Calvinist doctrines of the seventeenth century
offered an entire system for man's life and redemption, they
were not merely a list of rules or beliefs. Instead, one tenet
grew out of the other in a logical manner, and, therefore, the
doctrine of predestination, or election of the saints is
connected to the concepts of original sin and free grace.
Predestination offers an explanation for original sin. John
Bratt, in his attempt to explain Calvinist theology, claims
that the doctrine of predestination was popular in Christendom
during the seventeenth century and that the most controversial
doctrine was not predestination, but transubstantiation or the
"spiritual presence of Christ's body in the bread and wine of
communion."[13] Consequently, the doctrines of predestination
and election are mentioned frequently in the seventeenth-
century hymn. The hymns of Isaac Watts present a rich source
for such evidence. For example, in the following hymn, the
speaker thanks God for the opportunity to share the status of

64

Jesus, but more important to this study is the speaker's own
interpretation of the doctrine.

> Jesus, we bless thy Father's name;
> Thy God and ours are both the same;
> What heavenly blessings from his throne,
> Flew down to sinners through his Son!
>
> "Christ, be my first elect", he said,
> Then chose our souls in Christ our head,
> Before he gave the mountains birth,
> Or laid foundations for the earth.
>
> Thus did eternal love begin
> To raise us up from death and sin;
> Our characters were then decreed,
> Blameless in love, a holy seed.
>
> Predestinated to be sons,
> Born by degrees but chose at once:
> A new regenerated race,
> To praise the glory of his grace.
>
> With Christ, our Lord, we share our part,
> In the affections of his heart;
> Nor shall our souls be thence remov'd,
> Till he forgets his First Beloved.[13]

Contradicting the Biblical sequence of the creation and
attempting to establish the validity of predestination, the
hymn states that before the foundations of the earth were laid,
and before the land was formed, God chose his saints. The
Bible states that man is God's final creation (Genesis I, 26-
28). A few stanzas from yet another hymn by Watts will
demonstrate the belief that God's system of election is not
based on man's estate alone:

> But few among the carnal wise
> But few of noble race,
> Obtain the favor of thine eyes
> Almighty King of grace.

> He takes the men of meanest name
> For sons and heirs of God;
> And thus he pours abundant shame
> On honorable blood.
>
> He calls the fool and makes him know
> The myst'ries of his grace,
> To bring aspiring wisdom low
> And all its pride abase.[14]

These stanzas were probably intended to show God's
impartiality. God chooses for his heirs only few of noble
lineage. Obtaining God's favor, however, are men of lowly
birth. Even the fool, moreover, may be invited to learn the
mysteries of God's grace and the purpose of His dispensation.
He does not choose in the manner of worldly man, by power and
birth. Instead, God may slight the noble and elect the men of
"meanest birth" or even "fools" to enter into His kingdom.
These hymns have clear didactic purposes. In supporting the
election of the saints, they also encourage humility, another
Puritan tenet.

The concept that some persons are born for salvation and
others for damnation has eroded over the years, and stanzas
such as those quoted above no longer have relevance as
Presbyterian doctrine. Those hymns, however, which have
stanzas that deal with humility or God's saving grace have
survived regardless of any hints of out-worn doctrines. Two
stanzas from Isaac Watts's hymn, one of the most famous hymns
in English, will serve as an example here of such hymns that
have survived despite their overt, doctrinaire statements:

> When I survey the wondrous cross
> On which the Prince of glory died,
> My richest gain I count but loss
> And pour contempt on all my pride.
>
> Forbid it, Lord, that I should boast,
> Save in the death of Christ, my God;
> All the vain things that charm me most,
> I sacrifice them to his blood.[15]

Equally famous is John Newton's hymn "Amazing Grace," a good example of a hymn that has transcended the boundary of sacred song and is now a popular secular song:

> Amazing grace! how sweet the sound!
> That saved a wretch like me!
> I once was lost, but now am found
> Was blind, but now I see.
> 'Twas grace that taught my heart to fear,
> And grace my fears relieved;
> How precious did that grace appear
> The hour I first believed.
>
> Through many dangers, toils and snares,
> I have already come;
> 'Tis grace has brought me safe thus far,
> And grace will lead me home.[16]

This hymn as well as others by Newton constitutes his spiritual autobiography: his conversion from a slave ship captain to a hymn writer and minister. The first stanza of his hymn shows Newton's abject humility in calling himself a wretch. As severe as this term is, it has survived and is in current use in this hymn because the rest of the hymn demonstrates God's grace, a fundamental Calvinist doctrine.

In the Calvinist tradition, it was expected that the saints would face temptations but that they would persevere towards righteousness. Albert-Marie Schmidt explains that this method is used by God to make the pilgrim patient.[17] This doctrine is based upon the literal interpretation of the following Biblical passage:

> And not only so, but we glory in tribulations also; knowing that tribulation worketh patience and experience hope.
>   Romans 5:3-4.

Related to this concept is the belief that Christians lacking in perseverance displease God and, therefore, will be punished for their transgression.

Displaying the Calvinist doctrine of perseverance of the saints, in the canon of seventeenth-century hymns, is John Bunyan's Valiant's Song." This hymn typifies the major theme in the work of which it is a part, Pilgrim's Progress (1678). It states:

> Who would true Valor see,
> Let him come hither,
> One here will constant be,
> Come wind, come weather,
> There's no discouragement
> Shall make him once Relent
> His first avowed Intent
> To be a Pilgrim.
>
> Whoso beset him round
> With dismal storys
> Do but themselves confound,
> His strength the more is
> No Lyon can him fright,
> He'l with a Gyant Fight
> But he will have a right,
> To be a Pilgrim
>
> Hobglobin, nor foul Fiend,
> Can daunt his spirit:
> he knows, he at the end
> Shall Life Inherit.
> Then Fancies fly away,

68

> He'l fear not what men say,
> He'l labor Night and Day
> To be a Pilgrim[18]

Except for modern spelling, this version of the hymn is
similar to the original. The hymn promises a great reward for
the persevering pilgrim. It also declares a firm purpose of
achieving the goal of eternal life regardless of the
distractions of difficulties which may interfere with his
journey.

The hymn is of interest for a secondary historical reason
which may well be mentioned here. John Bunyan was drafted, at
age sixteen, into Cromwell's army. After the Restoration, he
was imprisoned for twelve years for disregarding the Act of
Uniformity. In 1672, he was released by the adoption of the
Declaration of Indulgence, but when his Declaration was revoked
three years later, Bunyan was imprisoned again.[19] Pilgrim's
Progress, in general, and a hymn such as "Valiant's Song"
reflect some of Bunyan's personal trials. Bunyan includes the
lines "No Lyon can him fight/He'l with a Gyant fight." These
lines can be interpreted as references to the King, the "Gyant"
whose royal crest was a lion. The final lines of that stanza
assert that one has a "right" to be a pilgrim.

With the hope that fear would spur the pilgrim onward, the
seventeenth-century hymn sometimes attempted to encourage
perseverance by showing God's anger. Isaac Watts's work
abounds in examples of hymns that perceive God as a God of

anger and wrath.   For example, after a thunderstorm on August

20, 1697, Watts wrote this hymn:

> Sing to the Lord, ye heavenly hosts;
> And Thou, O earth, adore:
> Let death and hell, through all their coasts
> Stand trembling at his power.
>
> His sounding chariot shakes the sky,
> He makes the clouds his throne;
> There all his stores of lightning lie
> Till vengeance darts them down.
>
> His nostrils breathe out fiery streams,
> And from his awful tongue
> A sovereign voice divides the flames
> And thunder roars along
>
> Think, O my soul, the dreadful day
> When this incensed God
> Shall rend the sky, and burn the sea,
> And fling his wrath abroad!
>
> What shall the wretch the sinner do?
> He once defy'd the Lord!
> But he shall dread the thunder now,
> And sink beneath his word.
> Tempests of angry fire shall roll'
> To blast the rebel worm,
> And beat upon his naked soul
> In one eternal storm.[20]

In some old hymns such as this one, God assumes the image of a

demonic or a Satanic figure to the modern reader. Watts's

purpose in using this image may have been to coerce the hymn

singer to follow the paths of righteousness. A versatile hymn

writer, Isaac Watts uses yet another technique, designed for a

similar purpose, in the hymn set forth below:

> Ye sons of Adam, vain and young
> Indulge your eyes, indulge your tongue,
> Taste the delights your souls desire,
> And give a loose to all your fire.

> Pursue the pleasures you design
> And cheer your hearts with songs and wine;
> Enjoy the day of mirth but know
> There is a day of judgment too,
>
> God from on high beholds your thoughts,
> His book records your secret faults;
> The works of darkness you have done
> Must all appear before the sun.
>
> The vengeance to your follies due
> Should strike your heart with terror through;
> How will ye stand before his face
> Or answer for his injur'd grace.[21]

Watts based this hymn upon the following Biblical reference:

> Rejoice, O young man, in thy youth; and let
> thy heart cheer thee in the days of thy
> youth, and walk in the ways of thine heart,
> and in the sight of thine eyes, but know thou
> that for all these things God will bring thee
> into judgment. (Eccl. XI, 9).

Watts used the structure of the hymn to help with the purpose.
The early stanzas are an invitation to worldly pleasures, but
the closing stanzas remind the Christian of the penalty of
those pleasures. This latter hymn is not as harsh as the
first cited, but it, too, depicts God as a God of Vengeance.

This concept of God was not limited to the English
Puritans. Jonathan Edwards, one of the earliest Puritan
preachers in America, has to his credit a sermon espousing the
same ideas. In the sermon "Sinner in the Hands of an Angry
God," Edwards asserts:

> The Bow of God's wrath is bent, and the Arrow
> made ready on the Sting and Justice bends the
> Arrow at your Heart, and strains the Bow, and
> it is nothing but the meer pleasure of God,
> and that of an angry God, without any Promise
> or Obligation at all, that keeps the Arrow

one moment from being made drunk with your
Blood.[22]

God is an "Angry God" who delights in punishing wrongdoers,

states Edwards. This theory is supported by yet another

American Puritan writer of the seventeenth century, Michael

Wigglesworth, those poem "The Day of Doom'" according to the

critics, is credited with being the most widely-read poem in

American during the seventeenth century. Two stanzas from part

three of this prodigiously long poem, "The Day of Doom," serve

to illustrate the fears of the seventeenth-century Puritan, as

well as the poet's vivid concept of Hell, and his portrayal of

the Angry God:

    203 What? to be sent to Punishment,
         and flames of Burning Fire;
         To be surrounded, and eke confounded
         with God's revengful ire.
         What? to abide, not for a tide
         these torments, but for Ever:
         To be released, or to be eased,
         not after years, but Never.

    205 They wring their hands, their caitiff-hands
         and gnash their teeth for terrour;
         They cry, they roar for anguish sore,
         And gnaw their tongues for horrour.
         But yet a way without delay,
         Christ pitties not your cry;
         Depart to Hell, their [sic] may you yell,
         and roar Eternally.[23]

In their stance on punishment for sin, these American Puritans

did not differ from the English Puritans.

    Counter to the idea of harsh punishment by God is the idea

of love and forgiveness. This idea coexisted with its opposite

in the seventeenth century. The following hymn by Herbert is addressed to an angry God, but it expresses a philosophy

contrary to that of Watts, Edwards, and Wigglesworth:

DISCIPLINE

Throw away thy rod,
Throw away thy wrath
  O my God,
Take the gentle path.

For my heart's desire
Unto thee are bent
  I aspire
To a full consent.

Not a word or look
I affect to own,
But my book
Any thy book alone.

Though I fail, I weep
Though I halt in pace,
  Yet I creep
To the throne of grace.

Then let wrath remove
Love will do the deed;
  For with love
Stonie hearts will bleed.

Love is swift of foot.
Love's a man of warre,
  And can shoot
And can hit from farre.

Who can 'scape his bow?
That which wrought on thee,
  Brought thee low,
Needs must work on me.

Throw away thy rod,
Though man frailties hath
  Thou art God.
Throw away thy wrath.[24]

In this hymn, Herbert makes a plea for mercy and lenience. The

hymn is a subtle criticism of the God of Wrath delineated in

some of the hymns of Watts. The poet suggest that there is a
flaw in God's system of punishment, and he suggests the law of
love as the corrective measure. At this stage the hymn becomes
revolutionary, for Puritans at that time accepted the Bible as
literal truth. The Bible says that "God is Love." Herbert is
metaphysical in his conceit comparing love with war and the
power of love to the action of artillery. These are disparate
ideas "yoked" together to create a richness of association,
typical of the metaphysical aspects of some seventeenth-
century hymns. Herbert extends the conceit successfully to
show the might and power of love. This hymn of Herbert's was
published verbatim in John Wesley's Collection of Psalms and
Hymns (1738).[25] It appears currently in the Oxford Hymn Book
as a general hymn with modernized spelling and with the third
stanza omitted. One may postulate that Stanza III is too
doctrinaire for current use since it supports the authority of
the Bible:

> Not a word or look
> I affect to won
> But by book
> And thy book alone.

Herbert's hymn demonstrates clearly one dilemma of the
seventeenth-century Puritans many of whom upheld the old law of
revenge and simultaneously ignored the new law of love. Yet,
Herbert vacillates, also, for in the following hymns, he
acknowledges both the angry God and the God of love by use of
paradox:

> Ah my Dear angry Lord!
> Since thou dost love yet strike
> Thou dost cast down, yet help afford
> Sure I will do the like.
>
> I will complain yet praise,
> Bewail, and yet approve,
> And all my other sowre-sweet Days
> I will lament yet love.[26]

Again, he writes of a God who slays and destroys, who desires

and disdains the wicked:

> Thou are God, whose purities
> Cannot in sin delight
> No evil, Lord, shall dwell with Thee,
> No fools stand in Thy sight.
>
> Thou hast those that unjustly do.
> Thou slayest the men that lie.
> The bloody man, the false one too
> Shall be abhorr'd by thee.
>
> Lord, lead me in thy righteousness,
> Because of all my foes;
> And to my dym and sinful eyes
> They perfect ways disclose.
>
> For wickedness their insides are,
> Their mouths no truth retain
> Their throat an open sepulchur
> Their flattering tongues do fain
>
> Destroy them Lord, and by their own
> Bad counsels let them fall
> In height of their transgression,
> O Lord, reject them all.[27]

The last stanza is a prayer that evil befall those who

transgress God's will. Again, the ironic posture of the poet

is revealed. This hymn is based upon the Fifth Psalm of David,

which asks for blessing for the righteous and curses for the

evil. By a selective process, however, Herbert focuses upon

the negative. It is likely that George Herbert wrote these

stanzas as a sincere prayer for the reason that psalms chosen
on particular occasions usually have relevance to that
occasion. For example, when Herbert mentions the "flattering
tongue," he may well be referring to the situation at the
English court. At that time, favors were generally dispensed
from the English court according to visible loyalty to the
monarch. At the base of Herbert's prayer, however, is a belief
akin to that of Watts that God will smite, reject, and destroy.

On the contrary, John Milton, himself a Puritan, chose to
praise the God of Love, and his hymn of praise has survived
throughout the ages; albeit Milton acknowledges God's knowledge
of the Puritans' "misery" and the human condition in general.

> Let us with a gladsome mind
> Praise the Lord, for he is kind
> For his mercies aye endure
> Ever faithful, ever sure.
>
> He hath, with a piteous eye,
> Looked upon our misery;
> All things living he doth feed,
> His full hand supplies their need.[28]

Based upon the literal interpretation of the Bible, this
confused situation did not deter the persistence in the belief
that the Bible was absolute authority. John Bratt, in his
discussion of the rise of Calvinism, points out that one of the
fundamental doctrines of Calvinism was the doctrine of the
"sufficiency of the Scripture." He explains that the doctrines
of salvation by faith and the sovereignty of God were secondary
to acceptance of the Bible as grounds for faith.[29]

Michael Walzer extends this notion further to include the
Calvinist belief that man's conscience is supported by fact,
that fact being the Bible, and he postulates the conscience, in
turn, gave magistrates and nobles the right to resist a king,
and, to declare "Godly warfare."[30] This conviction may have
formed the basis for the political behavior of the Puritans in
1642. This "Godly Warfare" is treated later in this book.

Several hymns of the seventeenth century support the theory
that the seventeenth century was an age of authority. Whereas
the Puritans accepted the Bible as their authority, the Roman
Catholics and Anglicans believed that mystical, divine
authority was given to the apostles and was passed on to
generations through apostolic succession. For example,
Dryden's old hymn, "That ancient fathers thus expound,"
contains the following stanzas that support this idea very
strongly:

> In doubtful questions, 'tis the safest way
> To learn what unsuspected ancients say;
>
> . . . .
>
> For 'tis not likely that we should higher soar
> In search of heaven, than all the Church before;
> Nor can we be deceived unless we see
> The Scriptures and the fathers disagree.
>
> Those truths their sacred words contain,
> The church alone can certainly explain
> The following ages, leaning on the past,
> May rest upon the Primitive at last.[31]

Although this hymn is not in common use, it echoes one of the
themes expressed in another Dryden hymn that is still popular

today. The hymn, "Creator Spirit by whose aid," originally
contained the following stanzas:

>Refine and purge our earthly parts.
>But, O, inflame and fire our hearts
>Our frailties help, our vice control,
>Submit the senses to the soul;
>
>And when rebellious they are grown,
>Then lay thy hand and hold them down
>Chase from our minds the infernal foe,
>And peace, the fruit of love, bestow;
>
>And lest our foot should step astray
>Protect and guide us in the way,
>Make us eternal truths receive
>And practise all that we believe.[32]

Dryden's personification of the senses has caused those stanzas
to be omitted from modern hymnals, but the third stanza has
been modified to read as follows:

>Plenteous of grace,d come from on high,
>Rich in thy sevenfold energy;
>Make us eternal truth receive,
>And practise all that we believe;
>Give us thyself, that we may see
>The father and the Son by thee.[33]

In instances such as these, one may look to the history of the
day for an explanation of the poet's motives and beliefs
expressed in hymn such as this. John Dryden, on the accession
of James II in 1685, became a Roman Catholic and remained one
for the rest of his life.[34] This fact is enlightening on two
counts. First, the idea that a man's religion may change
depending upon whom the English monarch may be seen shocking,
but change was common during the seventeenth century.
Secondly, any serious conversion to a new faith brings with it

moments of soul-searching, questioning, and justification.
Dryden, a Puritan, converted to Catholicism, experienced these
moments and naturally advanced Catholic doctrines in his hymns.
By doing so, Dryden reasoned with himself and confirms his
new-found beliefs, thus, his hymns assert respect for and faith
in ancient customs and beliefs. They show the influence of
seventeenth-century scholasticism and oppose the then current
custom of each man interpreting anew the Scriptures.

Additionally, the spiritual autobiographies of two other
great hymn writers reveal that they, too, experienced feelings
similar to Dryden's. John Bunyan, in his Grace Abounding to
the Chief of Sinners, explains his inner turmoil:

> Now I began to conceive peace in my Soul, and
> methought I saw the Tempter did lear and
> steal away from me, as being ashamed of what
> he had done . . . This gave me good
> encouragement for the space of two or three
> hours . . . but because it tarried not, I
> therefore sunk in my spirit under exceeding
> guilt again.[35]

Similarly, Cardinal John Henry Newman although not of the
seventeenth century writes in similar vein of his religious
turmoil:

> I felt then . . . that there was an
> intellectual cowardice in not having a basis
> in reason for my belief and a moral cowardice
> in not avowing that basis. I should have
> felt myself less than a man, if I did not
> bring it out, whatever it was . . . Alas!
> it was my portion for whole years to remain
> without any satisfactory basis for my
> religious profession, in a state of moral
> sickness, neither able to acquiesce in
> Anglicanism, nor able to go to Rome.[36]

Having its birth possibly in Cardinal Newman's time of decision, his universally acclaimed hymn "Lead Kindly Light" grew from his contemplation to be converted to Roman Catholicism. He eventually converted in 1845 but by his own admission had "whole years of contemplation". On the other hand, Dryden's hymn, written in 1963, eight years after his conversion may be interpreted, therefore, as his public testimony, or as a reinforcement of his faith.

Whereas Dryden's hymn points to "unsuspected ancients" as the authority, Isaac Watts and other Independents insisted on the literal interpretation of the Bible. For example, in a hymn for youth, Watts inserted the following stanzas advancing the belief in the purity of the Bible:

> But still thy law and Gospel, Lord,
> Have lessons more divine.
> Not earth stands firmer than Thy Word,
> No stars so nobly shine.
>
> Thy word is everlasting truth;
> How pure is every page!
> That holy Book shall guide our youth
> And well support our age.[37]

Again, a forthright affirmation of the absolute authority of God's word appears in the following stanzas:

> Our nation reads the written Word,
> That book of life that sure record;
> The bright inheritance of heaven
> Is, by sweet conveyance, given.
>
> God's kindest thoughts are here express'd,
> Able to make us wise and bless'd;
> The doctrines are divinely true,
> Fit for reproof and comfort too.
> Ye people all, who read his love

> In long epistles from above,
> (He hath not sent his sacred Word to every land,)
> praise ye the Lord.

Watts again writes of the Sufficiency of the Bible and

denounces other factual avenues to truth:

> The sacred words impart
> Our Makers just commands;
> The pity of his melting heart,
> And vengeance of his hands.
>
> . . . .
>
> We learn Christ crucify'd
> And here behold his blood;
> All arts and knowledges beside.
> Will do us little good.
>
> In vain shall Satan rage
> Against the book divine
> Where wrath and lightning guard the page
> Where beams of mercy shine.[38]

To Isaac Watts, revelation of God's commands is restricted to

the pages of Holy Writ, and clear principles of truth and life

are to be found in specific examples and texts of the Holy

Scriptures. He goes to the extreme to denounce all "other arts

and knowledges" as being to man of little good. Ignorant of

the foundations of arts and knowledge and reluctant to

contemplate the effect of these entities on human life, Watts

and others exclude themselves from a level of thought achieved

by the more metaphysical writers many of whom were in accord

with the Cambridge Platonists. This particular hymn is not in

common use, probably because of its extreme point of view, but

several of Watts's hymns expressing the authority of the Bible

have survived.[39]

Other hymn writers have honored the Word of God in hymns, but few are as doctrinaire as Watts. William Cowper, for instance, among his <u>Olney Hymns</u>, has written such a hymn in which the following stanzas appear:

> A Glory guilds the sacred page,
> Majestic like the sun;
> It gives it light to every age
> It gives but borrows none.
>
> The hand that gave it still supplies
> the Gracious light and heat:
> His truths upon the nations rise
> They rise but never set.
>
> Let everlasting thanks be thine
> For such a bright display.,
> As makes a world of darkness shine
> With beams of heavenly day.[40]

Here, Cowper's sun simile suggests that the word of God enlightens, but his hymn is not as dogmatic and narrow as the hymns of Watts. Providing the base for some of the finest English hymns of later years, the doctrine of the Bible as authority has become so richly integrated with poetic skill that the modern hymn singer tends to extract the spiritual essence of hymns and to neglect the structural foundation, in much the same way that one tends to be inspired by the beauty of a great cathedral without noticing that it is structurally wood, stone, and steel. One example of such a hymn is William How's "O Word of God Incarnate," quoted in its impressive entirety here:

> O Word of God incarnate,
> O Wisdom from on high,
> O Truth unchanged, unchanging,

O Light of our dark sky;
We praise thee for thy radiance
That from the hallowed page
A lantern to our footsteps,
Shines on from age to age.

The Church from her dear Master
Received the gift divine,
And still that light she lifteth
O'er all the earth to shine
It is the golden casket
Where gems of truth are stored;
It is the heav'n-drawn picture
Of Christ, the living Word.

It floateth like a banner
Before God's host unfurled;
It shineth like a beacon
Above the darkling world;
It is the chart and compass
That o'er life's surging sea
Mid mists and rocks and quicksands,
Still guides, O Christ, to Thee.

Oh, make thy church, dear Savior,
A lamp of purest gold,
To bear before the nations
Thy true light as of old,
Oh teach thy wand'ring pilgrims
By this thy path to trace,
Till clouds and darkness ended,
They see thee face to face.[41]

A hymn as comprehensive as this one seems to have drawn
from both the Puritan and the Catholic doctrines. Its
superiority to the older hymns rests in its language and also
in its more sophisticated meter. One must bear in mind,
however, that Watts wrote approximately two hundred years
earlier than How, and, as Bernard Manning explains, even
between Watts and Addison language differences may be observed,
and he describes the differences thus:

When Watt's taste was set the English

> language had not undergone that purging and
> purifying, that rationalization and
> simplification, which we associate with the
> name of Addison. Here we find a contrast
> between Watts and Wesley. Watts's forbears
> wrote crabbed, allusive, tortuous prose and
> verse. Charles Welsey's forbears wrote the
> slick polished stuff.[42]

The modern students of hymnology cannot afford to base their
observations of hymns merely on their refinement. They often
have to go beyond the form to the substance. When this is done
they find that Isaac Watts and some of the older hymn writers
still emerge as the writers of first-rate hymns. Henry
Vaughan, for example, developed his hymns mainly through the
application of metaphors, some elaborate and sustained, others,
simple and homely. These hymns having a marked relationship to
Vaughan's life are somewhat explained by a knowledge of that
life.

During the Civil War (1642-1646), Henry Vaughan was opposed
to combat. He, therefore, did not take an active part in the
war. His brother Thomas, however, entered the war and fought
for the king. During the Puritan interlude, a Parliamentary
Ecclesiastical Commission was set up to conduct inquisitions.
Thomas Vaughan was expelled from his church and was later
arrested on the charge of having "bourne arms for the king."
Henry Vaughan was subsequently imprisoned for his attachment to
King Charles II.[43] The modern scholar can hardly avoid the
inference, therefore, that several of Vaughan's hymns and
metaphors may have been composed with particular people and

84

circumstances in mind. For example, Henry Vaughan writes of
the church as follows:

>Ah! He is fled!
>And while these here
>Their mists and shadows hatch
>My glorious Head
>Doth on those hills
>Of Myrrhe and Incense watch.
>
>Haste, haste, my dear!
>The souldiers here
>Cast in their lots again,
>That seamless coat
>The Jews touch'd not
>These dare divide and stain.[44]

These stanzas are important because of the allusions that
Vaughan makes. First, the speaker suggests that God is absent,
and in his absence a conspiracy has taken place. The inclusion
of "soldiers" suggests that the conspiracy is of a military
nature and will lead to fighting. Next, there is a reference
to the Crucifixion of Jesus:

>And they crucified him, and parted his
>garments, casting lots; that it might be
>fulfilled what was spoken by the prophets,
>they parted my garment among them, and upon
>my vesture did they cast lots.
>   St. Matthew 27:35

The garment, the seamless coat, represents the universal
church, and the dividing of the garment symbolizes the factions
into which the church had split. The scholar of seventeeth-
century literature will recognize the similarity between the
above reference and Swift's prose satire, "A Tale of a Tub,"
written about 1696. In this work, the author tells of a father
who leaves a coat as his legacy to each of his three sons:

Peter, Martin, and Jack. He willed that on no account should the coats be altered. The sons disobey their father's will. Soon Martin and Jack quarrel with the proud Peter, and then with each other, and they separate. The satire is against Peter (from Peter, first Bishop of Rome), the symbol of the Roman Catholic Church and its doctrines; Martin (from Martin Luther), the symbol of the Anglican church, and Jack (from John Calvin), the symbol of the dissenters.[45]

Another effective metaphor that Vaughan uses to represent the fragmented state of the Church and religion is the metaphor of a pure stream becoming polluted, and instead of a religion being a "physick:" it becomes a "disease."[46] The metaphor is particularly suitable to that age. A seventeenth-century churchman could readily comprehend such a homely reference: religion should be a "physick" and purge men's souls, but as he perceived it, the polluted stream of religion was spreading disease. That is to say, persons, who partook of that water, the water of life, had, instead, an unclean religion that could lead to spiritual death. On several levels, therefore, Vaughan's references may be interpreted as references to political, social, and religious conditions in his life and, by extension, to the trials of life, in general.

Henry Vaughan was not singular in expressing his personal concerns in hymns. Richard Baxter another major hymn writer (1615-1691) shared his concerns also. One of his hymns, still

in common use, voices concern over the fragmentation of the
church thus:

> He wants not friends that hath thy love,
> And may converse and walk with thee
> And with thy saints here and above,
> With whom for ever I must be.
> In the communion of [thy] saints
> Is wisdom, safety and delight;
> And when my heart declines and faints,
> It';s raised by their heat and light.
>
> As for my friends, they are not lost;
> The several vessels of thy fleet,
> Though parted now, by tempests, tost,.
> Shall safely in the heaven meet.
>
> Still we are centred all in thee ,
> Members, though distant, of one Head;
> In the same family we be,
> By the same faith and Spirit led.
>
> Before thy throne we daily meet
> As joint-petitioners to thee;
> In spirit we each other greet,
> And shall again each other see.
>
> The heavenly hosts, world without end,
> Shall be my company above;
> And thou, my best and surest Friend
> Who shall divide me from thy love?[47]

Baxter is comforting himself that all the various denominations
have "one Head" and, moreover, he is rationalizing his loss of
earthly friendships because of religious differences. He,
nevertheless, consoles himself by acknowledging God as his
"best and surest friend."

Bluntly expressed in several seventeenth-century hymns,
doctrinaire ideas probably had a clear purpose of teaching and
explaining. The didactic hymn was accepted then. Thus, the
zealous congregation was frequently instructed in the Christian

theology upon which their church was founded. Millar Patrick

gives the following explanation of the situation.

> The discovery was made early in the Christian
> era that popular religion is moulded largely
> by the ideas enshrined in its hymns. Sermons
> fly over people's heads; prayers uttered in
> their name often fail to carry their hearts
> and even their intelligence with them; but
> their songs sing into the memory, color their
> thoughts, and fashion much more than any
> deliberate instruction.[48]

Church goers are often captivated by the simplicity, the

rhythm, and the emphasis found in hymns. Sometimes the

doctrine of the seventeenth-century hymns, however, was mostly

dogma.

John Mason Neale translated several of the great Latin

hymns and they, too, contained direct doctrines. Overton in

his appraisal of Neale's work found that:

> The Roman Catholics accused him [Neale] of
> deliberate deception because he took no pains
> to point out that he had either softened down
> or entirely ignored the Roman doctrines in
> those hymns . . . As, however, the
> translation were intended for the use of the
> Anglican Church, it was only to be expected
> that Neale should omit such hymns or portions
> of hymns as would be at variance with her
> doctrines and disciplines.[49]

Yet, much of Neale's translations would seem strongly Roman

Catholic to today's scholar. For example, the following

stanzas translated from St. Ambrose by Neale clearly illustrate

veneration The Virgin Mary:

> Come, Thou Redeemer of the earth,
> Come, testify Thy Virgin-birth:
> All lauds admire; - all things applaud;

> Such is the birth that fits a GOD
>
> . . . .
>
> The Virgin womb that burden gain'd
> With Virgin honour all unstain'd:
> The banners there of virtue flow:
> God in His temple dwells below.
>
> . . . .
>
> Proceeding from His Chamber free,
> The royal hall of chastity,
> Giant of twofold substance, straight
> His destined way He runs elate.
>
> . . . .
>
> All honour, laud, and glory be,
> O Jesus, Virgin-born to Thee!
> All glory, as is ever meet,
> To father and to Paraclete.[50]

In this hymn, a strong Roman Catholic tenet is exhibited.
The dogma is expressed that Jesus is as much to be honored
because of the status of his mother, The Virgin Mary, as he is
to be honored for the status of his Divine Father.

Using mostly seventeenth-century hymn writers, Martha
England explains the position of the doctrinal hymn as follows:

> Watts, Herbert, Milton, T. S. Eliot--all were
> careful of doctrine, conscious of image and
> symbol . . . The doctrines differed . . . In
> a given poem, the demand for recognizing the
> relations of that poem to the Bible may be
> met in different ways. Watts rested the
> weight of his hymns and psalms on doctrinal
> interpretation as contrasted with literal
> which had been the ideal of earlier church
> music. His method gave to his best work, a
> grandeur of generalization that is
> unsurpassed in hymnody.[51]

Watts's hymns, however, reflect a doctrinal interpretation,

based on the literal meaning instead of the mere doctrinal ones
suggested by England. Further, it is this interrelationship of
doctrine and Scripture that gives to Isaac Watts's hymns much
of their general appeal.

In discussing religion and its place in hymns, Edgar
Newgrass points out the inevitability of incorporating church
doctrine in hymns:

> Denominations cannot be ruled out of
> hymnology anymore than out of religion . . .
> Any honest approach to Deity, and efforts to
> follow the teachings of the Master--teachings
> which permeate hymnology as well as
> Scripture--is to be honoured. In point of
> fact, the various denominations have much
> more in common than there is dividing them.
> How frequently indeed do hymn writers of
> different denominations express each in his
> own way, the same helpful idea.[52]

Newgrass' idea is realistic because the didactic hymn may be so
subtle that no congregation would object to it. For example,
the popular hymn "The Church's One Foundation," quoted here in
part, is one of the most doctrinaire hymns in the English
language. It speaks for itself in these stanzas:

> The Church's one foundation
> Is Jesus Christ her Lord;
> She is his new creation
> By water and by word:
> From heav'n he came and sought her
> To be his holy bride;
> With his own blood he thought her,
> And for her life he died.
>
> Elect from ev'ry nation
> Yet one o'er all the earth
> Her charter of salvation,
> One Lord, one faith, one birth;
> One holy Name she blesses,

> Partakes one holy food,
> And to one hope she presses,
> With ev'ry grace endued.
>
> Though with a scornful wonder,
> Men see her sore opprest,
> By schisms rent asunder,
> By heresies distrest;
> Yet saints their watch are keeping,
> Their cry goes up, "How long?"
> And soon the night of weeping
> Shall be the morn of song.[53]

In stanza I, the hymn advances a very strong Roman Catholic
tenet that the Church is the "holy bride" of Christ. Also,
reference is made to the creation of the church through the
practice of Baptism and through the apostolic word or the words
of the Bible. Continuing in the same vein, stanza two
acknowledges the universality of Christianity and suggests
particular Christian practices such as Holy Communion,
sovereignty of God and hope for salvation. The third stanza
turns to the mundane problems of the Church, the fragmentation
through heresy. In this stanza, also, there is mention of the
old Puritan practice of saints keeping watch for the second
coming of Christ. Despite the presence of religious dogma in
this hymn, it has survived because its acceptable doctrines are
presented in agreeable terms. On the contrary, Isaac Watts's
hymn advancing Christ as a bridegroom has not survived because
of its colloquial language. Utilizing Song of Solomon IV.1, 10
and 11, the opening stanzas of Watts' hymn exemplify the entire
hymn:

> Kind is the speech of Christ our Lord,

> Affection sounds in every word:
> "Lo, thou art fair, my love," he cries,
> "Not the young doves have sweeter eyes."
>
> "Sweet are thy lips; thy pleasing voice
> Salute mine ear with secret joys;
> No spice so much delights the smell.
> Nor milk nor honey, tastes so well."
>
> "Thou are fair, my bride, to me;
> I will behold no spot in thee;"
> What mighty wonders love performs,
> And puts a comliness on worms!"[54]

The framework of Watts's hymn is a dialogue of a secular love scene. Although Watts attempts to incorporate the same idea expressed in "The Church's one foundation," his hymn fails because it is unpoetic. Watts's crude stanzas lack dignity and carry sensual connotations in the key words. Yet, in another context, the concept of a Christian being married to the church is accepted quite readily.

The evidence demonstrates that regardless of the tastes of the age, some hymns which reveal church doctrines survive. Hymns which express agreeable doctrines such as the Holy Trinity are held in highest esteem. Partially explaining the seventeenth-century practice of hymn writers expressing their strongest motivations in hymns, Louis Benson observes that "a great hymn is the fullest embodiment of Christian Doctrine.[55] It seems, then, that the presence of church doctrine in a hymn does not mar that hymn, but rather it is the manner in which the doctrine is expressed, consonant with the status and current acceptability of that doctrine that determine the

92

hymn's acceptance or rejection.

NOTES FOR CHAPTER III

[1]Michael Walzer, The Revolution of the Saints (Cambridge, Mass: Harvard University Press, 1965), p. 27.

[2]The Baptist Hymnal (Philadelphia: The American Baptist Publication Society, 1920), No. 204.

[3]It is important to note that in early American poetry the same practice of promulgating religious dogma prevailed. For example, Michael Wigglesworth's poem "In Adam's fall/We sinned all" carries the same idea.

[4]The Baptist Hymnal, No. 223.

[5]Bailey, Gospel in Hymns, p. 58.

[6]John Donne, The Complete Poetry and Select Prose of John Donne, ed. John Haywood (New York: Random House, 1941), p. 272.

[7]Saunders, Evenings With the Sacred Poets, p. 230.

[8]The English Hymnal (London: Oxford University Press, 1933), No. 515.

[9]Henry Vaughan, Sacred Poems, p. 111.

[10]Isaac Watts, Psalms, Hymns and Spiritual Songs (Cincinnati: Corey and Webster, 1836), No. 57.

[11]John Chrysostom, Manual of Christian Doctrine (Philadelphia, Pennsylvania: John Joseph McVey, 1902), p. 355.

[12]John Bratt, The Rise and Development of Calvinism: A Concise History (Grand Rapids, Michigan: William B. Eerdmans Publishing Co., 1959), pp. 27-28.

[13]Isaac Watts, Psalms, Hymns and Spiritual Songs, No. 54.

[14]Watts, Psalms, Hymns and Spiritual Songs, No. 96.

[15]The Baptist Hymnal, No. 442.

[16]The Church Hymnary: A Collection of Hymns and Tunes for Public Worship, Edwin Bedell, comp. (New York: Maynard, Merrill, and Co., 1893), No. 552.

[17]Albert-Marie Schmidt, John Calvin and the Calvinist

<u>Tradition</u>, trans., Ronald Wallace (New York: Harper & Brothers, 1960), p. 122.

[18]<u>The Clarendon Hymn Book</u>, No. 297.

[19]Ryden, <u>The Story of Christian Hymnody</u>, p. 258.

[20]Watts, <u>Psalms, Hymns and Spiritual Songs</u>, Book II, No. 62. The note on this hymn verifies the fact that Isaac Watts was writing hymns before the eighteenth century. His first book of Hymns was published in 1707 and most of his hymns are given that date or a later one. Additionally, for almost every hymn in his collection, Watts has stated the doctrine upon which the particular hymn is based, and he often gives the passages of Scripture upon which the doctrine rests, thereby suggesting divine inspiration through the Scripture.

[21]Watts, <u>Psalms and Hymns</u>, Book I, No. 89.

[22]Jonathan Edward, "Sinners in the Hands of an Angry God" in <u>The Literature of the United States</u>, Vol. I, eds., Walter Blair <u>et al</u> (Chicago: Scott, Foresman and Co., 1953), p. 198.

[23]Michael Wigglesworth, "The Day of Doom," <u>The Literature of the United States</u>, Vol. I, p. 222.

[24]Francis T. Palgrave, <u>The Treasury of Sacred Song</u> (Oxford: Clarendon Press, 1889), p. 49.

[25]John Julian, <u>Dictionary of Hymnology</u>, p. 1175.

[26]<u>Select Hymns Taken Out of Mr. Herbert's Temple and Turn'd into Common Metre to be Sung in the Tunes Ordinarily Us'd in Churches</u> (London: S. Bridge, 1697), pp. 28-29.

[27]Edward Farr, <u>Select Poetry, Chiefly Sacred of the Reign of James I</u> (Cambridge: Cambridge University Press, 1745), No. xii.

[28]<u>The Clarendon Hymn Book</u>, No. 214.

[29]John Bratt, <u>The Rise and Development of Calvinism</u>, p. 29.

[30]Michael Walzer, <u>The Revolution of the Saints</u>, p. 60.

[31]Saville, <u>Lyra Sacra: Being a Collection of Hymns Ancient and Modern</u>, Rev. B. W. Saville, compiler (London: Longman, Green, London and Roberts, 1861), p. 255.

[32]Saunders, <u>Evenings with the Sacred Poets</u>, p. 266.

[33]*The Hymnal of the Protestant Episcopal Church* (New York: The Church Pension Fund, 1940) No. 371 and *The English Hymna No. 156.*

[34]Routley, *Hymns and Human Life*, p. 169.

[35]John Bunyan, *Grace Abounding to the Chief of Sinners* ed. Roger Sharrock (Oxford: Clarendon Press, 1962), p. 44.

[36]John Henry Newman, *Apologia Pro Vita Sua* (London: Oxford University Press, 1913), p. 166.

[37]*Evangelical Lutheran Hymn-Book* (St. Louis, Missouri: Concordia Publishing House, 1927), No. 112.

[38]Watts, *Psalms, Hymns and Spiritual Songs*, Book I, No. 53, and Book II, No. 120.

[39]See *The Baptist Hymnal*, Nos. 6, 78, 79, 220, 222, and the *Evangelical Lutheran Hymn-Book*, Nos. 114 and 115 for samples.

[40]*The Baptist Hymnal*, No. 219 and John Newton, *The Olney Hymns* (Burlington: Isaac Neale, 1785), No. 19.

[41]*The Hymnal of the Episcopal Church*, No. 402.

[42]Bernard Manning, *The Hymns of Wesley and Watts: Five Informal Papers* (London: The Epworth Press, 1942), p. 82.

[43]H. F. Lyte, ed. *Vaughan's Sacred Poems and Pious Ejaculations* (London: George Bell and Sons, 1890), p. xix.

[44]Lyte, *Vaughan's Sacred Poems*, p. 40, and *Clarendon Hymn Book* No. 293.

[45]*The Oxford Companion to English Literature*, p. 798.

[46]Vaughan, *Sacred Songs,* p. 32.

[47]*The Clarendon Hymn Book*, No. 190.

[48]Ernest E. Ryden, *Christian Hymnody*, p. vii.

[49]John Julian, *Dictionary of Hymnology*, p. 788.

[50]John Mason Neale, *Collected Hymns* (London: Hodder and Stroughton, 1914), pp. 104-105.

[51]Martha England and John Sparrow, *Hymns Unbidden* (New York: New York Public Library, 1966), p. 76.

96

[52]Edgar Newgrass, <u>Melody in Your Heart: A Concise History of Hymnology</u> (Bushey Heath, Hertfordshire: A. E. Callam, 1964), pp. 9-10.

[53]<u>The Protestant Episcopal Hymnal</u>, No. 396.
[54]Isaac Watts, <u>Psalms, Hymns and Spiritual Songs,</u> Book I, No. 73.

[55]Louis Benson, <u>Hymnody of the Christian Church</u> (New York: George H. Doran Co., 1927), p. 146.

CHAPTER IV

POLITICS, WAR, AND PEACE IN THE
SEVENTEENTH-CENTURY ENGLISH HYMN

The association of politics, war, and peace with religion
and thus with the history of English hymns dates back to the
Reformation of the sixteenth century. Protestant reform led by
Luther was not peaceful; for not only did he attack the life of
the Roman Catholic church, but he attacked the teachings as
well. Luther questioned time-honored beliefs such as the
infallibility of the pope and the ability of man to play a role
in forgiveness of sins through the purchase of pardons. In
England, the Reformation of the church was more political than
elsewhere because of the combination of church and state and,
also, because of the blood relationships of English monarchs to
Scottish and French rulers - each embracing different aspects
of Protestantism.

The accession of the Stuart kings to the English throne was
accompanied by the new doctrines of High Church and Divine
Right of Kings, both unpopular with the freedom-loving English
people. Urged to conform to the authority of the established
Church of England, Non-conformists and Independents refused to
honor the king's codes. In 1629 King Charles I dissolved
parliament. This upheaval in the political life of England was
directly related to upheavals in practices and structure of the
Church. Lay, religious movements challenged established ones

and this resulted in alterations in the social and political
life of England. While the ecclesiastical structures were
breaking, the religious life was gradually quickening and a
man's religion became, at once his politics, too. The
supporters of the sovereign were labelled "Royalists," and the
faction favoring the power of parliament became known as
"Parliamentarians." While the monarch ruled single-handedly,
he increased all abuses, and the feud grew more intense.

For reasons of trade and commerce, political cohesiveness
and religious freedom, among others, most Puritans adhered to
the principles of parliamentary government. To have done
otherwise would have exposed them to the mercies of a
tyrannical sovereign and his Star Chamber whose chief members
were Lord Buckingham, the Earl of Strafford and Archbishop
William Laud.

From among the parliamentarians, Oliver Cromwell, a Puritan
leader arose. In 1642, Civil War erupted. Within two years
the Royalists were beaten, and in 1649 King Charles I was
beheaded, dying as a traitor and a tyrant.

Describing the aftermath, John R. Green writes of Cromwell,
the new Lord Protector:

> In England, Cromwell dealt with the Royalists
> as irreconcilable enemies, but in every other
> respect he carried fairly out his pledge of
> healing and settling . . . The anarchy which
> had reigned in the Church since the breakdown
> of Episcopacy . . . was put to an end by a
> series of wise and temperate measures . . .
> Save in his dealings with the Episcopalians,

whom he looked on as a political danger,
Cromwell remained true to the cause of
religious liberty.[1]

Writing of himself, however, in a letter to his brother,

Richard, who was Mayor of Hursley, Cromwell in 1650 states,

"when I write to the Parliament, I usually am, as becomes me,

very particular with them and usually from thence the knowledge

thereof is spread."[2]

It was not enough for the Puritans to effect a change in

government or a shift in the ruling power. Whatever evil they

thought had been done, they set about to undo. In March 1641,

Archbishop Laud was arrested, and was executed in 1645. Percy

Dearmer captures the spirit of the times in his description

below:

> On the day of Laud's arrest, . . . a
> committee was appointed which demanded the
> demolition of the altars, candlesticks,
> pictures, images, vestments and the ornaments
> . . . The organs were burnt, the stained
> glass windows smashed, the churches used to
> stable horses.[3]

Dearmer goes on to explain that Will Dowsing, a Cromwellian

government agent, was paid six shillings and eight pence for

each church destroyed. At Queen's Chapel at Cambridge, for

example, he "beat down one hundred and ten superstitious

pictures besides chirubims." At Peterhouse, he "pulled down

two mighty great angells with wings, and diverse other angells

and the four Evangelists, and Peter . . . over the Chapell

Dore, and about one hundred chirubims.[4]

For the purpose of this study, it becomes necessary to explain that Puritanism in the seventeenth century was not merely a development in the spiritual life of the English. It was, an outgrowth of the Reformation and became a political evolution. Both inside and outside the Established Church, Puritan ideals were held. According to Erik Routley, Puritanism constituted a political party that in "1612 was oppressed and exiled, in 1640, openly rebellious, in 1649 victorious, and in 1662 punished, but always fighting."[5] Ideologically, Puritans identified with the Biblical Children of Israel. The caption, Puritan embraced all those sects that opposed the order and worship of the Anglican Church, another legal designation of which was the Established Church of England. The term Puritan applied to such sects as Independents, Separatists, Congregationalists, Presbyterians, Baptists and all others that strove for a purer and simpler form of worship than that of the Established Church.

Because of the political situations that led to the Civil War of 1642, it is not surprising to find several seventeenth-century hymns relating to warfare or political strife. Even when no actual battles raged, the images and references to war and fighting still appeared in the hymnody of the times.

Providing a rationale for the military state of affairs mentioned above were two puritan doctrines. The first was based on the belief that God sanctioned any army that defended his cause, because man's first obedience was to God and not to any legal, man-made code. Government should be by the "collective elect" and not by a sovereign monarch.[6] This position dates back to the Reformation when the fundamental points of disagreement related to the doctrine of man. Luther had attacked the teaching that man can perform good works and pay indulgences to atone for his sins. Above all Luther had denied the infallibility of the Pope. Now, a century later, the English found that their monarchs were reverting to powers formerly held by the Pope.

Secondly, Puritans held that persecution was a means whereby patience could be taught.[7] Consequently, they viewed much that was undesirable as training situations for their spiritual life. The Civil War was viewed as "Godly warfare." It was the former belief that led the Scottish Puritans in 1643 to effect a return to a pure form of worship and to sign the covenant from which they got their name, the Covenanters. They made the following pledge:

> By the great name of the Lord, our God, to
> continue in the profession of obedience of
> the said religion, and that we shall defend
> the same, and resist all their contrary
> errors and corruptions according to our own
> vocations and the utmost of that power which
> God has put into our hands all the days of
> our life.[8]

Many seventeenth-century hymns soothe the Christian spirit, inspire the mind or praise the greatness of God,[9] but in addition to the foregoing, the repertory of seventeenth-century hymns, like most others, contains its share of hymns of war and action. These are hymns which team with vigorous human life and, in some cases, tell the story of the age in which they were born.

According to Millar Patrick the Puritans sang hymns, but scholars are not sure what hymns they sang. It is accepted, however, that the Puritan demand for "literalness" led them to sing translations of psalms that accurately served their purpose. One such psalm used under Oliver Cromwell is Psalm LXVII regularized for chanting and freed of obscurity:

> Let God arise, and scattered
> Let all his enemies be;
> And let all those that do him hate
> Before his presence flee.[10]

In fact, this psalm was the rally cry to which Cromwell turned when faced with perplexity during his attack upon the Scottish forces. Bad August weather had diminished the English forces and Cromwell held a devotional service about four o'clock one afternoon. The historian Guizot recounts the details as follows:

> The English spent the night in noiseless
> preparations for combat. The night was wild
> and wet . . . . At the outset the English
> had the worst of it . . . the fight continued
> hotly for sometime, amid cries of "The Lord
> of Hosts!" from the English, and "The
> Covenant!" from the Scots. At about seven
> o'clock, Cromwell's own regiment of foot
> charged suddenly and broke the Scottish
> lines. At this moment the fog dispersed, the
> sun shone brightly over hill and ocean.
> "Now, let God arise," exclaimed Cromwell,
> "and his enemies shall be scattered!" His

words gave fresh courage to his men, and were
chanted by all who stood near him . . . .
Enthusiasm is as contagious as
discouragement; the English charged with
redoubled vigor; the Scottish cavalry gave
way.[11]

Cromwell himself wrote of this battle: "After the first
repulse, they were made by the Lord of Hosts as stubble to our
swords."[12]

Cromwell and the Puritans marched into battle singing
psalms. Quoted, in part, below are sections of the Seventy-
Sixth Psalm, chanted by the Covenanters who fought against
Royalist forces led by Lord Claverhouse at Drumclog:[13]

> In Judah is God known . . .
> There brake he the arrows of the bows
>   the shield, and the sword, and the battle.
> Thou art more glorious and excellent than
>   the mountains of prey.
> The stout-hearted are spoil'd. They have slept
>   their sleep and none of the men of might have
>   found their hands . . .
> Thou, even thou, art to be feared:
>   and who may stand in they sight when
>   once thou art angry?
> He shall cut off the spirit of princes:
>   he is terrible to the kings of the earth.
>   (Ps. 76)

Selected because of its appropriateness for battle, this
Psalm makes specific reference to kings and princes of earth,
who, the Covenanters believed, were the source of all their
problems.

Many of the Psalms treat the theme of war, as, in fact,
they deal with the war-like activities of King David and,
consequently, the metrical psalm fulfilled the spiritual and

political needs for Puritan action. Native hymns, however,
superseded those psalms and are the hymns of war and wrath.
One of the oldest hymns is the current National Anthem of
Britain. Scholars are uncertain of its origin, its date, and
its patron, but John Julian traces it to the seventeenth
century, and dates it about 1688 since copies of it were common
among the Jacobites.[14] Agreeing with Julian, Paul Harvey
states that in all likelihood "the song was written in favor of
James II in 1688 (when the invasion by the Prince of Orange was
threatening) or possibly, of Charles II in 1681."[15] In its
earliest version, the anthem was composed of two stanzas. In
its earliest entirety, however, it is as follows:

> God save our Lord, the King.
> Long live our noble king
>   God save the king!
> Send him victorious
> Happy and glorious
> Long to reign over us,
>   God save the king.
>
> O Lord, our God, arise
> Scatter his enemies
> And make them fall.
> Confound their politiks
> Frustrate their knavish tricks
> On him our hopes are fixed
>   O save us all.

The more civilized third stanza was added during the rational
age of the eighteenth century.

> Thy choicest gifts in store
> On him be pleased to pour,
>   Long may he reign.
> May he defend our Laws,
> And ever give us cause
> To sing with heart and voice

God save the king.[16]

The anthem is important because of the explicit diction and the loyal attitude expressed. It expresses the thought that the sovereign is supreme and that the subjects are satisfied with him. It asks God to defend the king by scattering his "enemies." Consequently, the diction of Stanza II is explicit in its use of verbs such as "scatter," "confound," "fall" and "frustrate." These are warlike words of action. Contrasted with Stanza II, the stanza imploring defeat, Stanza I uses positive words such as "save," "live," victorious," "reign" and "noble," representing victory. Because of its images the hymn succeeds in portraying the polemics and partisan mood of the times. Arthur Pollard points out, that if a hymn is to be successful, the hymn writer must use familiar images. Novelty is a distraction in hymns.[17] This hymn serves two functions with respect to the argument of this book. First,, the familiar seventeenth-century image of political enemies planning "knavish tricks" was real to the people of that age. In addition, the notion that God would assist the king demonstrates the accepted doctrine of the Royalists who, of course, believing in the Divine Right of kings, logically concluded that God would protect them against their enemies and adversaries. Secondly, the hymn reveals to the modern scholar the polemical spirit of the seventeenth century.

It seems safe to postulate that on the theme of war, the

metrical psalm clearly influenced the hymn. Psalms such as the
Seventy-Sixth quoted earlier express the theme of war; and even
in the paraphrases of psalms of praise that are set to music,
recognition is given to God as God of war. One such example
showing that God will defend His people is taken from Nahum
Tate's Psalter of 1688:

> O praise ye the Lord, prepare your glad voice
> His praise in the great assembly to sing;
> In their great Creator let all men rejoice
> And heirs of salvation be glad in their king.
>
> With glory adorned, His people shall sing
> To God who defence and plenty supplies
> Their loud acclamations to him their great king
> Through earth shall be sounded and reach to the
> skied.[18]

Exhibited here are the ideas of praise as well as the idea that
God is a defender. An important observation, however, is that
in The Church Hymnal of the Protestant Episcopal Church in the
United States of America, this psalm appears as a hymn with
only slight changes and without any notation of its Biblical
origin. It is written thus:

> Oh praise ye the Lord! prepare your glad voice
> His praise in the great assembly to sing:
> In their great Creator let Israel rejoice;
> And children of Zion be glad in their King.
>
> With glory adorned, His people shall sing
> To God, who their heads with safety doth shield;
> Such honor and triumph His favor shall bring
> O, therefore for ever all praise to him yield.[19]

Sung to the tune "Hanover" or better known as "O Worship the
King," the hymn asserts that God supplies defense in times of
war, a prospect overlooked neither by the psalmist or the

translator.

Among the earliest hymn writers of the seventeenth century stands George Wither (1588-1643), in whose work can be found some of the best examples of the invasion of the hymn by politics. Although Wither vacillated in his support of the king, most of his hymns reflect very strong Royalist tendencies. Other poems in his "Collection of Emblems" are considered metaphysical in nature. George Wither's name is very important in hymnology, however, because he published, though faced with many odds, the first English hymn book. Partisan that he was, in 1623, Wither obtained from James I a patent for his Hymnes and Songs of the Church to be bound with each copy of the metrical Psalter.[20] The Company of Stationers was angered and protested against Wither's profiteering in the word of God. "They declared the hymns to be popish, superstitious, obscene, and unfit to keep company with David's psalms." Furthermore, they felt that "such writing should be left to clergy."[21] To this accusation, George Wither replied in a pamphlet, "The Scholar's Purgatory," with a counter accusation:

> Those metrical psalms were never commanded to
> be used in divine service, or in our public
> congregations, by any canon or ecclesiastical
> constitution, though many of the vulgar be of
> that opinion. But whatsoever the stationers
> do in their title page pretend to that
> purpose.[22]

Wither's charge was ignored, and the stationers' attack

realized its projected intent of disallowing Wither to popularize his hymn book.

The social, political, and religious impact of Wither's hymn book, Hymns and Songs of the Church, is a source of scholarly disagreement. Evaluations of the hymns vary, but the following discussion represents both sides of the question. Louis Benson claims that Wither's "hymns faded into oblivion."[23] On the contrary, Gillman claims that Orlando Gibbons set several of Wither's hymns to music and that they became popular.[24] The student of hymnology will find Dr. Benson's statement extreme. For although the original work was barred from circulation, Wither republished his work in 1641 under the title of Hallelujah or Britain's Second Remembrancer.[25] Also, it is possible that Wither's hymns were made available in manuscript form. In addition, several of Wither's hymns survive today. Three well-known ones are "The Lord of Heaven Confess" (Clarendon Hymn Book, No. 278 "Behold the sun that seemed till now" (Oxford Hymn Book, No. 16), and "Come O come, in pious lays" (Clarendon Hymn Book, No. 167). The latter appears to have been a likely source for Watts's later hymn "Come, let us join our cheerful songs." Wither's hymns have enjoyed more popularity than those of Benjamin Keach, for example. Both men wrote approximately three hundred hymns, yet none of Keach's hymns seem have survived into succeeding centuries.

Wither, a frail supporter of the king, dedicated his
Hymnes and Songs of the Church to "the high and mighty Prince
James by the grace of God, King of Great Britain, France,
Ireland. Defender of the Faith."[26] Julian points out that
Wither's work represents the "signs of the times when the
balance of power between the king and parliament hung even . .
. [when] the great struggle was opening and will be seen in the
many hints and suggestions." He goes on to classify Wither's
work as that of "a waverer on the border of two camps."[27]

Wither's "Victory" and "Peace" hymns are not listed in
contemporary hymnals, but they serve best to demonstrate the
fact that some seventeenth-century hymns were warlike. In the
following hymn "Victory", God is given the credit:

> We love thee, Lord, we praise they name
> Who by thy great almighty arm
> Has kept us from the spoil and shame
> Of those that sought our causes harm,
>
> Thou are our Life, our Triumph-Song
> The joy and comfort of our heart
> To thee all praises do belong
> And though the Lord of Armies art.
>
> We must confess it is thy power
> That made us master of the field
> Thou art our Bulwark and our Tower
> Our rock of refuge, and our shield.
>
> Thou taught'st our hands and arms to fight
> With vigor thou did'st gird us round
> Thou mad'st our foes to take their flight
> And thou did'st beat them to the ground.
>
> To blood and slaughter fiercely bent,
> And perils round did us inclose
> By whatsoever way we went
> That had'st not thou or Captain been,

> To lead us on and off again
> We on the place had dead been seen
> Or masked in blood and wound had lain.
>
> This song we therefore sing to thee
> And pray that thou for ever more
> Wouldest our Protector daigne to be
> As at this time and here to fore
> That thy continual favor shown,
> May cause us more to thee incline
> And make it through the world be known
> That such as are our foes are thine.[28]

The action in this hymn is convincing and its structure
supports its meaning. Gradually gaining momentum, the hymn
moves from a simple statement or praise to starkly realistic
images of God leading troops on and off the battlefield, or
enemies bent to "blood and slaughter," and of wounded troops
strewn over the scene. Wither's "Song of Peace" is more
gruesome in its representation of war. Depicting images from
seventeenth-century civil war, Wither's hymn "Peace" is not
suited to the poetry of hymnody, especially that which
celebrates life and peace. It must be admitted, however, that
the hymn celebrates the fact that these circumstances did not
occur:

> No troops the ploughman fears,
> No shot our walls o'er return,
> No temple shakes about our ears,
> No village here doth burn.
>
> No father hears his pretty child,
> In vain for succor cry.
> No husband sees his wife defiled
> While he half-dead doth lie.
>
> So cause us, Lord to think upon
> Those blessings we possess,
> That what is for our safety done

We truly may confess.
For we, whose fields in time forepast
Most bloody war did stain.[29]

Cicely V. Wedgewood attempts to explain Wither's realistic

style in hymns such as the foregoing one as follows:

> From the outbreak of the war even more poets
> who were highly skilled in the fashionable
> manner of the 1630's adopted a simple, even
> crude form of writing when their intention
> was to defend a cause--usually the king's--to
> as wide a public as possible . . . Such
> developments meant death to the elegance and
> delicacy of the previous decade, though grace
> and courtliness did not immediately vanish.[30]

Certainly, Wither's bizarre images of fearful ploughmen,

burning villages, crying children, violated women, and beaten

men appealed to the most untutored minds and now present

reasons for the demise of such hymns. Other hymns by Wither

clearly show his political bias and they demonstrate the true

nature of the seventeenth-century hymn. For example, he writes

a hymn especially for the king. To the twentieth-century

critic, the dedication of that hymn might seem to be solicitous

and fawning, but in its day it constituted the matter of which

loyalty was made. The dedication reads:

> For the benefit of the Commonwealth receiveth
> by the Prince to pray for his preservation
> also, and to desire a blessing upon him and
> his Government: To which purpose this song
> is composed.

The hymn reads:

> When, Lord, we call to mind those things
>   That should be sought of Thee,
> Remembering that the heart of Kings
>   At thy disposing be;

> And how of all those blessings, which
> Are outwardly possest:
> To make a kingdom safe and rich,
> Good princes are the best.
>
> . . . .
>
> Let neither Partie Struggle from
> That duty should be shown,
> Let each to other plagues become,
> And both be overthrowne:
> For o're a disobedient Land,
> Thou dost a Tirant set
> And those that Tyrant-like command,
> Have still with Rebels met.
>
> Oh, never let so sad a doome
> Upon these Kingdoms fall,
> And to assure it may not come,
> Our sinnes forgive us all:
> Yea, let the parties innocent
> Some damage rather share,
> Then, by unchristian discontent,
> A double curse to bear.[31]

Demonstrating the fact that in a partisan age citizens held

positions based upon their religious and political beliefs,

this hymn also shows that there were others, nevertheless, who

were conciliatory. Such were the Cambridge Platonists,[32] led

by Lord Herbert of Cherbury and Henry Moore. Although Wither

dedicates the hymn to the king, and despite the fact that the

Stanza I reaffirms the doctrine of Divine Right Kings, the hymn

writer states that both parties owe a duty to England. Let

each become a plague visited upon the other if either neglects

its duty to England. Especially does Wither condemn tyranny.

Without stating that Charles I was a tyrant and that he,

indeed, commanded rebels, wither leaves a political loophole

for himself. The author of <u>Abuses Stript and Whipt</u> postpones

the evil outcomes to a time that may not come and assumes the
guise of politician turned penitent. Playing his political
hand with adroit circumspection, the hymn writer invokes
"damage," or condemnation, upon the innocent, the non-
participating bystanders who with "unchristian discontent" must
bear a double curse, meaning a curse from Puritan
parliamentarians and radicals alike. Hardly a better example
may be found to demonstrate the seventeenth-century hymn as a
mode for sacred and secular matters.

Proceeding in a carefully reasoned and bi-partisan spirit,
Wither states that love is the blessed cement that will bind
the broken parts of the kingdom, for polemics, fire, and sword
are immiscible and cannot blend in the binding power of love.
They are the weapons of malice that are mutually beguiling to
those who think that paper warfare, fire, and sword can ever
unite the religious and political factions in England. Wither
pleads for peace and love in this hymn.

> Love is that blessed Cymment, Lord,
>   Which us must reunite,
> In bitter speeches, fire, and sword,
>   It never took delight:
> The weapons those of Malice are,
>   And they themselves beguile:
> Who dreame that such ordained were
>   Thy Church to reconcile.
>
>   . . . .
>
> No longer let Ambitious Ends,
>   Blind Zeale, or cankered Spight,
> Those Churches keep from being Friends
>   Whom love should fast unite:
> But let thy glory shine among

114

> Those Candlesticks we pray,
> We may behold what hath so long
> Exil'd thy Peace away
>
> . . . .
>
> That those, who (heeding not thy Word)
> Expect an Earthly Powre,
> An vainley thinke some Temprall Sword
> Shall Antichrist devoure;
> That those may know, thy weapons are
> No such as they doe faigne
> And that it is no Carnall Warre
> Which we must entertain.[33]

Building a case as it were, against stark factionalism,
blind zeal, and cankered spite, the hymn writer pleads to God
that these cantankerous partisans not be permitted to continue
to keep disunited the church that should be bound in love.
Continuing in penitential spirit, the hymn writer pleads that
the glory of the spirit of God will shine among the
candlesticks in place of dim candlelight, so that this bright
spiritual light may disclose the darker images of the first
stanza: bitter speeches, fire, and sword. In this well
reasoned hymn, Wither asserts that there are Englishmen who
think that a temporal soldier-king will devour Antichrist, that
is to say, the Catholic or anti-establishment factions. Not
so, says Wither, pleading that partisans may come to know that
God's weapons are not polemics, war, and political faction, but
love, instead; for it is not a war against man that is being
waged but against the powers of darkness. Wither's celebrated
contemporary, the partisan polemicist, John Milton, was guilty
of most of these strictures. A critical reading of these hymns

establishes Wither as a voice of reason in these partisan
times, using the hymn as a mode of expressing moderate
political views.

Although John Milton (1608-1674), the leading seventeenth-
century Puritan poet, is well-known as a hymn writer, mention
must be made of his works that relate directly to the civil
strife of his day. Milton held the important position of Latin
Secretary to the Commonwealth. After the execution of Charles
I Milton published two papers, "The Tenure of Kings and
Magistrates" (1649) and "Eikonoclastes" or "Imagebreaker"
(1649), in which he refutes Bishop John Gauden's "Eikon
Basilike," a work accepted then to be meditations of Charles I.
In addition, Milton published "Pro Populo Angelicano Defensio"
(1651) and "Defensio Secunda" (1654).[34] For these works that
were considered anti-Royalist and strongly Puritan, Milton was
arrested at the Restoration but later regained his freedom.
Even when the persecution of Protestants took place in Europe,
Milton felt compelled to speak against such slaughter. What is
now considered one of his most famous sonnets, "Avenge, O Lord,
thy Slaughtered Saints," was written when the Italian Duke of
Savoy massacred his protestant subjects.[35]

A brief excerpt from Milton's "Tenure of Kings and
Magistrates: The Readie and Easie Way to Establish a Free
Commonwealth" serves to show his strong disapproval of the
doctrine of Divine Rights of Kings:

116

> . . . For Divines, if ye observe them, have
> their postures, and their motions no less
> expertly, and with no less variety than they
> that practice feats on Artillery-ground . . .
> But if there come a truth to be defended,
> which to them, and their interest of this
> world seems not so profitable, straight these
> nimble motionists can finde no eev'n leggs to
> stand upon . . . if we return to Kingship . .
> . as undoubtedly we shall, when we begin to
> find the old incroachments coming on by
> little and little upon our consciences, which
> must necessarily proceed from King and Bishop
> united inseparably in one Interest, we may be
> forc'd perhaps to fight over again all that
> we have fought . . . for our Freedom.[36]

To the political situation in England, Milton also
responded in poetry. Unlike Wither's, Milton's verses are
direct and bold. Names are mentioned, and praise as well as
grievance is expressed as is seen in his poem, "On the New
Forcers of Conscience under the Long Parliament":

> Because you have thrown off your Prelate Lord
>   And with still Vowes renounc'd his Liturgie
>   To seise the widdow'd whore Pluralite
>   From them whose sin ye envi'd, not abhor'd,
> Dare ye for this adjure the civill Sword
>   To force our Consciences that Christ set free,
>   And ride us with a classic Hierachy
>   Taught ye by meer A. S. and Rutherford?
> Men who Life, Learning, Faith and pure intent
>   Would have been held in high esteem with Paul
>   Must now be nam'd and printed Hereticks
> By shallow Edwards and Scotch and what d'ye call:
>   But we hope to find out all your tricks,
>   Your plots and packing wors then those of Trent,
>   That so the Parliament
>   May with their wholsom and preventative Shears
>   Clip your Phylacteries, though bauk [sic] your
>   Ears,
>   And succor our just Fears
> When they shall read this clearly in your charge
> New Presbyter is but Old Priest write Large.[37]

Succinctly stating the Puritan cause, Milton points out in this

poem the evils of the Anglican Church.[38] He states in the
first line that the Church of England has thrown off the Papal
power, but it has taken the form "Pluralite" for mere
convenience. Referring to Henry the VIII who, in his opinion,
sinned, Milton complains that the civil authorities dare to
control the consciences of men. Further, he opposes the system
of incarceration meted out to men who dissent. He hopes that
the ignoble intent of his political opponents will be exposed
so that Parliament will regain control, and thus "clip" the
power of the monarch, showing that the "New Presbyter," or new
form of religion, is no different from the "Old Priest" or the
Catholic tradition.

To this poem, one might add three others that deal with the
Civil War: "To My Lord Fairfax," "To OLiver Cromwell," and "To
Sir Henry Vane." These pieces laud the virtues of each man,
but contain passages that reveal Milton's deep concern for the
state of the nation: In "Lord Fairfax," Milton questions the
folly of war:

> For what can War, but Acts of War still breed,
> Till injur'd Truth from Violence be freed;
> And publick Faith be rescued from the Brand
> Of publick Fraud: In vain doth Valour bleed,
> While Avarice and Rapine shares the Land.[39]

Again, in the poem "To Oliver Cromwell" he writes of

religious freedom:

> Yet much remains
> To Conquer still, Peace hath her Victories
> No less than those of War; new Foes arise
> Threatening to bind our Souls in secular chains,
> Help us to save Free Conscience from the paw,

Of Hireling Wolves, whose Gospel is their Maw.[40]

According to Greene, even Milton's longer poetic works are of historical importance. <u>Paradise Lost</u>, he claims, is the epic of Puritanism. Its theme is the problem of sin and redemption, evil against good, with which the Puritan wrestled in hours of gloom and darkness. He continues to explain that the vile rabble in <u>Comus</u> represents the men who trod underfoot Milton's "cause."[41]

It must be remembered that John Milton held a most important and influential position in the religious and political life of his times. Identifying his own political and religious views with God's cause and the course of righteousness, Milton supplies much of the rationale and substance of the seventeenth-century hymn. His hymn "Mercy and Truth" demonstrates the foregoing statement:

> Mercy and Truth that long were missed
> Now joyously are met;
> Sweet peace and righteousness have kissed
> And hand in hand are set.
>
> Truth from the earth, like to a flower,
> Shall bud and blossom then
> And Justice from her heavenly bower
> Look down on mortal men.[42]

What Milton expressed in poetry and prose, he and other seventeenth-century hymn writers often expressed in hymns in which one is likely to see the speaker, like Samson of "Samson Agonistes," living a "Life in captivity/Among inhuman foes."[43]

Sometimes, the theme of war is expressed through protest

against its dangers and aftermath. The seventeenth century had
no extended periods of peace and, worse yet, the wars were
civil ones that constantly exposed the English people to the
physical reality of war. Because of civil strife, moreover,
families were often divided to the point of open hostility.

Strong protest against the war was voiced by the
metaphysical poet and hymn writer, Henry Vaughan, whose hymn,
"Peace," is still sung in many churches in its original
arrangement. With modernized spelling, the hymn appears in the
Clarendon Hymn Book as a general hymn:

> My soul, there is a country
> Far beyond the stars,
> Where stands a winge'd sentry
> All skillful in the wars.
>
> There above noise, and danger,
> Sweet peace sits crowned with smiles,
> And one born in a manager
> Commands the beauteous files.
>
> He is thy gracious friend.
> And -- O my soul, awake! --
> Did in pure love descend,
> To die here for thy sake.
>
> If thou canst get but thither,
> There grows the flower of peace,
> The Rose that cannot wither,
> Thy fortress and thy ease.
>
> Leave then thy foolish ranges,
> For none can thee secure
> But one, who never changes,
> Thy God, thy life, thy cure.[44]

This hymn has metrical irregularities, including a third
stanza which does not fit the metrical pattern of the rest of
the hymn. Set to music during the seventeenth century, the

musical score of the hymn shows that Stanza III is made up of
four regular lines with six beats fitted to the tune, with
dashes taking the space of the extra beat.

The hymn makes use of metaphors and personifications that
combine to give it a tone quite expressive of its title,
"Peace." In the presence of "sweet Peace," or the never-fading
flower, Peace, the hymn writer urges the factions to leave
"foolish ranges" (matters) in quest of security in the presence
of God who never changes. "Cure," the final word of the last
stanza, is the strongest. It is a religious word (Latin: cura,
ae, English: care, cure), a pastoral assignment or curate, the
resident clergyman who takes care of the church. This peaceful
hymn, on close reading, discloses a protest against the Civil
War and advocacy of a haven above the noise and danger of the
times, where the king, unlike Charles I, is a gracious friend
and protector.

Replete with martial and political images, consonant with
civil strife in England, the hymn mentions, in Stanza IV, "The
Rose," that is to say, the king who was related to the
Lancastrian dynasty whose royal symbol was a red rose and whose
fortresses stood about England. Seek, instead, the stanza
counsels, the king of heaven who will assure spiritual comfort
in an abiding fortress.

Postulating that Henry Vaughan wrote hymns in "protest
against the tyranny and persecution suffered under Cromwell and

the Puritans."[45] Francis M. Palgrave points to Vaughan's hymn,

"The Men of War" as an example of such a hymn. Henry Vaughan's

experience during the Civil War is fully discussed elsewhere;;

therefore, the hymn will be examined:

>Who with a sword doth others kill
>A sword shall his blood likewise spill.
>Here is the patience of the Saints,
>And the true faith which never faints.
>
>. . . . .
>
>For in thy bright instructing verse
>Thy Saints are not the conquerors,
>But patient, meek and overcome
>Like thee, when set at naught and dumb.
>
>. . . . .
>
>But seeing soldiers, long ago,
>Did spit on thee and smite thee too,
>Crowned Thee with thorns, and bowed the knee,
>But in contempt, as still we see;
>
>I'll marvel not as ought they do
>Because they used my savior so;
>Since of my Lord they had their will,
>Thy servants must not take it ill.
>
>Dear Jesus, give me patience here,
>And faith to see my crown as near
>And almost reach'd because 'tis sure
>If I hold fast and slight the lure.
>
>Give me humility and peace
>Contented thoughts, innoxious ease,
>A sweet, revengeless, quiet mind
>And to my greatest haters kind.[46]

In The Treasury of Sacred Song, the first stanza, overtly

doctrinaire, is not included in the hymn. The missing stanza

is constructed upon the old philosophy of retribution, or an

"eye for an eye." Vaughan points out the irony of the fighting soldier-saint of his day and the patient, meek saints of the Scriptures. Although this is not a literal interpretation, the hymn, nevertheless, ends on a trusting note, reassuring the world that revenge is not of God.

On close examination, the reader observes that Vaughan points to atrocities such as the cruelties that Jesus endured prior to His Crucifixion. No less than the war atrocities alluded to by Wither in his hymn, "Peace," these activities mentioned by Vaughan do not seem crude or unsuited to hymnody because the hymn of this superior poet is more polished. Beginning with the theme of vengeance, the poem progresses in a logical, argumentative tone to humility and peace, revealing more poetic sophistication than Wither's hymn. These qualities explain, in part, its presence in contemporary hymnals and the absence of Wither's hymn, which, in seeking a wide contemporary audience, sacrificed dignity of style, and, consequently, missed the immortality often accorded a canon of hymns.

The political situation of the seventeenth century helps to shed light on a group of hymns which speak mainly of the Christian's contentedness. It appears that several hymn writers, desiring not to appear partisan, concentration on Christian life and its hopeful aspects. In addition, there seems to be a correlation between the hymn writer's political affiliation and his degree of contentedness. John Bunyan, a member all his life of the oppressed Puritan faction, provides

a good illustration of the hymn writer's ability to relate
political affiliation to spiritual contentedness. In the hymn
"He that is down needs fear no fall," popular in its original
form today, Bunyan expresses in Stanza II his contentment:

> I am content with what I have,
> Little be it or much;
> And, Lord, contentment still I crave
> Because thou savest much.[47]

Louis Benson states that "Bunyan wrote no hymns by intent"
and that what he wrote was confined to his "co-religionists."[48]
Yet, Bunyan's hymn, mentioned here, was excerpted from
Pilgrim's Progress (1684) and set to music by Jeremiah Clark
(c.1669-1707), a circumstance that suggests the strong
possibility that the poem became popular as a hymn during the
seventeenth century. In the earlier editions of Pilgrim's
Progress, Bunyan, more poetaster than poet, uses his hymns as
links between the chapters, joining the action, exhorting
Christian in his journey to the Celestial City, or warning him
of dangers along his pathway.

On the contrary, Richard Baxter (1615-1691), a leading
Puritan and outstanding hymn writer of the day, wrote hymns for
congregational singing. Testifying to this intent are his
numbered stanzas and the specific reference that Baxter made to
the psalm tune appropriate for the hymn.[50] In his Poetical
Fragments with Sacred Hymns, for example, Baxter makes the
following note for the hymns:

> For Creation, Redemption, the Holy Ghost and

124

> Sanctification, Pardon and Justification,
> Church Providence, Promised Glory, God's
> Word. The Communion of the Saints . . . To
> the Tunes of the old 51 and 100 Psalms: but
> leaving out the words in the Italic Letter,
> they may be sung in very many shorter Psalm-
> tunes in Psalms, and Hymns, and Spiritual
> Songs, singing with grace in your hearts to
> the Lord." Col.. 3.16.[51]

Examined along with the fact that in 1622 Baxter was
ejected from the ministry of his Presbyterian church as a
result of the Act of Uniformity, Baxter's hymns are of special
importance.

Richard Baxter was more than superficially concerned with
the struggles of his day. To gain a brief insight into his
contribution to the religious life of the seventeenth century,
one must examine some of his prose writings. In his work
entitled, "The cure of Church Divisions," for instance, he
discusses, in detail, the problem of division in the Church.
Baxter notes that division hinders "quiet and comfort of
spirit, freedom of spirit, sweetness of communion." Division
also obstructs the productive use of Christians' "time,
prayers, [as well as] their gifts and their graces." He
further claims that division causes the sins of "violation of
the law of love, dishonour of Christ, hindrance of the Prayer
of Christ, grief of the spirit of God, offence of our brethren,
corruption, hardening in sin, and hindrance to others in
finding God's Way." Baxter continues to give the "Cures of
Division" in the following order: "Peace and Love will

reconcile differences. Strife will not gain what love can. It is better to do good than to receive it. Other men's good is ours as well as theirs. Our good is more in the public good than ourselves -- the Golden Rule. To yield is more honorable than to overcome." Finally, he asks his fellow countrymen to consider "the love of God, the fellowship of men, the differences of men, the will of God - peace, the presence of God and Christ, their own weakness and mortality and the final account."[52] Noting "peace" as the first remedy for strife, Baxter pleads accordingly:

> What God hath done for peace with us, calls aloud to us to prize peace one with another . . . If it cost Christ his life to make our peace with God, we should be willing to do anything we are able, even to the hazard of our lives, to make peace among the saints . . . Remember, God hath called us to peace. That case upon which the apostle mentions our calling to peace, is as difficult to preserve peace in, as any can fall out in one's life . . . but it must be, saith the apostle, and grounds it upon this, God hath called us to peace.[53]

Not as explicit as his prose, Baxter's hymns show some traces of political factionalism. Overriding the political hints, however, is a tone of quiet resignation. If one bears in mind that the Act of Uniformity had set rigid constraints upon ministers and possible punishment for non-compliance with these orders, and that Baxter had chosen to dissent, his hymn "Lord, it belongs not to my care" may be interpreted against the troubled, ecclesiastical scenario of the times:

>Lord, it belongs not to my care
>   Whether I die or live;
>To love and serve thee is my share
>   And this thy grace must give.
>
>If life be long, I will be gland
>   That I may long obey:
>If short, yet why should I be sad
>   To welcome endless day?
>
>Christ leads me through no darker rooms
>   Than he went through before:
>He that unto God's Kingdom comes
>   Must enter by this door.
>
>Come, Lord, when grace has made me meet
>   Thy blessed face to see;
>For if thy work on earth be sweet,
>   What will thy glory be!
>
>Then shall I end my sad complaints
>   And weary sinful days,
>And join with the triumphant saints
>   To sing Jehovah's praise.
>
>My knowledge of that life is small,
>   The eye of faith is dim,
>But 'tis enough that God knows all,
>   And I shall be with him.[54]

Since political executions and imprisonments were common during the seventeenth century, Stanzas I and II of Baxter's hymn could well be a hint at the reality of life and death, but he leaves the matter to God's grace. Baxter, in Stanza II, compares his lot to that of Christ and concludes with the Puritan thought that one requirement for entrance to heaven is suffering that purifies. In yet another hymn, "He wants not friends that hath thy love," Baxter makes an indirect hint at the political actions of the Puritans:

>He wants not friends that hath thy love,
>   And may converse and walk with thee

And with thy saints here and above,
    With whom forever I must be.

In the communion of the saints
    Is wisdom, safety and delight;
And when my heart declines and faints,
    It's raised by their heat and light.

And for my friends they are not lost;
    The several vessels of thy fleet,
Though parted now, by tempest tost,
    Shall safely in the haven meet.

Still we are centered all of thee,
    Members, though distant, of one Head;
In the same family we be,
    By the same faith and spirit led.

Before thy throne we daily meet
    As joint-petitioners to thee,
In spirit we each other greet,
    And shall again each other see.

The heavenly hosts, world without end,
    Shall be my company above;
And thou, my best and surest Friend,
    Who shall divide me from thy love?[55]

With a very slight hint of his lack of friends, Baxter
makes the basic theme of this hymn the doctrine of communion of
the saints in this world and in the world to come, a favorite
theme of seventeenth-century hymn writers. Wisdom, safety
probably from political and personal danger, and delight are to
be found in this communion. Continuing the theme of communion,
and with still another political hint, Baxter asserts that
although his friends are buffeted by tempests and travel in
"several" vessels, they shall all meet with him in the safe
haven, that is to say, heaven.

Always, nevertheless, the saints are centered in God. It

is possible, in this third stanza, to interpret the hymn to
mean that Baxter and his Puritan co-believers, sailing the seas
in search of religious liberty, will meet, at last, in a safe
political place, presumably the American colonies or other
Puritan havens. The fifth stanza lends itself to a political
interpretation in an age when citizens either singly or jointly
stood before the king's throne with petitions, but the
religious impact of the closing lines is inescapable. The hymn
is a discourse on the heavenly kingdom with possible references
to contemporary problems of the earthly one.

Almost identical to Baxter's hymn is John Austin's
"Blest be thy love." Austin also wrote with the intent that
his hymns be sung. He was but two years younger than Baxter,
and he, too, a minister, had witnessed the Puritan Interlude as
well as the Restoration. Like Baxter's, Austin's hymn shows
quiet resignation:

> Blest be thy love, dear Lord,
>   That taught us this sweet way,
> Only to love thee for thyself,
>   And for that love obey.
>
> O thou, our soul's chief hope,
>   We to thy mercy fly;
> Where'er we are, thou can'st protect;
>   Whate'er we need, supply.
>
> . . . .
>
> Whether we live or die,
>   Both we submit to thee,
> In death we live, as well as life,
>   If thine in death we be.[56]

Showing a close similarity to Baxter's hymn, "Lord it belongs not to my care," Austin's hymn also espouses the idea that the Christian's role is to love and serve God, and that since everlasting life belongs to those who do accordingly, it does not matter whether "we live or die."

To write a hymn on content may well be synonymous to accepting publicly the fact that the hymn writer's political mentor has been successful. In the case of George Wither, for example, Simonds reports that Wither sold his property to purchase horses for Cromwell's Army.[57] Such an extreme act of loyalty should, in the seventeenth century, foster contentment, and possibly inspire a hymn such as the following, called the "Author's Hymn" by Wither, suggesting that it was his personal sentiments that were being expressed:

> By thy grace, those passions, troubles,
>   And those wants that me oppress't
> Have appeared as water bubbles
>   Or as dreams, and things in jest:
> For, thy leisure still attending,
>   I, with pleasure, saw their ending.
> Those afflictions and those terrors
>   Which to others grim appear,
> Did but show me where my errors
>   And my imperfections were;
> But distrustful could not make me
>   Of thy love, nor fright nor shake me.[58]

The hymn writer thanks God for attending to his wants, his troubles and his passions, but more important, in the second stanza, he makes reference to the "afflictions" and "terrors" of others. Not shaken nor frightened, his only realization is that he, being imperfect was prone to err. Failing to regard the Puritan or Royalist acts as grim or terrible, Wither felt politically secure with the government, whichever it was.

Not peculiar to the English hymn of the seventeenth century, the militaristic themes and images pervade much of Christian hymnody. As early as 720 AD Andrew of Crete wrote the following hymn which was rendered into English by John Mason Neale in the nineteenth century:

> Christian dost thou see them
> On the holy ground,
> How the powers of darkness
> Rage thy steps around?
> Christian up and smite them,
> Counting gain but loss;
> In the strength that cometh
> By the holy cross.
>
> Christian, dost thou feel them
> How they work within
> Striving, tempting, luring,
> Goading into sin?
>
> Christian, never tremble,
> Never be down-cast;
> Gird thee for the battle
> Thou shalt win at last.[59]

Aware of the constant warfare that a Christian wages against evil, the hymn uses terms that apply to war. It speaks of the armed camps and the darkling stealthy enemy ready to engage in fighting. The warlike verbs assure the Christian soldier that although there may be casualties, his strength lies in marching in the vanguard of the holy cross. Turning next to man's constant warfare with sin, the hymn writer assures the Christian that if he remains steadfast and fearless, he will be victorious. Admittedly, this is not a seventeenth-century hymn in the strictest chronological sense, but its warlike spirit is seventeenth century, nevertheless.

Still popular, Isaac Watts's hymn "Kingdoms and thrones to God Belong" perpetuates the theme of warfare:

> Proclaim Him King, pronounce Him Blest;
> He's your defence, your joy, your rest;
> When terrors rise, and nations faint
> God is the strength of every saint.[60]

The stanza, quoted here, contains the sole reference to warfare, but an examination of the source of the hymn reveals matters relevant to this study. In its original seventeenth-century version, the hymn read in its opening stanza:

> Let God arise in all his might,
> And put the troops of hell to flight;
> As smoke that sought to cloud the skies
> Before the rising tempest flies.[61]

The stanza beginning "Kingdoms and Thrones" was the sixth stanza, and the one first quoted was originally the ninth stanza. Reaching even beyond the seventeenth century, however, this hymn had its foundation in the Psalms. Psalm LXVIII begins as follows:

> Let God arise, let his enemies be scattered:
> let them also that hate him flee before him.

Apparently, one of the more popular psalms, it appeared in 1561 in the Sterhold and Hopkins Psalter. In 1650, almost a hundred years later, it was retained in Tate and Brady's New Version The English Psalter. In the latter version, the first line is changed to read "Let God, the God of battle rise."[62] Whatever the variation, the attitude of the hymn writer remains constant whenever the hymn deals with war. Always a conqueror, God is

132

always assumed to be on the side of the Christian fighting for
his cause in a war made holy by His presence, in a war made
just by His sanction, in a war made right by His victory.
Supporting this postulation, a paragraph from Oliver Cromwell's
letter to his brother justifies the Puritan victory thus:

> Only this let me say, which is the best
> intelligence to Friends that are truly
> Christian: The Lord is pleased still to
> vouchsafe us His presence, and to prosper His
> own work in our hands, -- which to us is more
> eminent for truly we are a company of poor
> weak worthless creatures. Truly our work is
> neither from our own brains nor from our
> courage and strength: but we follow the Lord
> who goeth before, and gather what he
> scatterth . . . We have taken many
> considerable places lately, without much
> loss. What can we say to these things! If
> God be for us who can be against us?[63]

Just as Oliver Cromwell did, the hymn writers of the earlier
ages gave God certitude, vastness, power, and praise while they
made soldiers of Christians. In so doing not only do they
reflect the sentiments of their age, but they also emphasize
the concept that Christians are constantly at war with
temptation.

Influencing later hymnody, the seventeenth-century hymns
that deal with war leave marks on a number of hymns that seem
to fulfill the militaristic tradition. The characteristics of
the seventeenth-century hymns in this tradition are the
militaristic images of God, the kingly captain, the Christian
soldier armed with sword, the necessity of the soldier's
watchfulness, prayer, and confidence that the struggle will

bring forth rich rewards. Displaying all these characteristics simultaneously, Isaac Watts's hymn, "Am I am solider of the cross"[64] exemplifies the typical seventeenth-century hymn of this category:

> Am I a soldier of the cross,
>   A follower of the Lamb?
> And shall I fear to own his cause
>   Or blush to speak His Name?
>
> Must I be carried to the skies
>   On flowery beds of ease,
> While others fought to win the prize,
>   And sailed thro' bloody seas?
>
> Are there no foes for me to face?
>   Must I not stem the flood?
> Is this vain world a friend to grace,
>   To help me on to God?
>
> Sure I must fight if I would reign;
>   Increase my courage, Lord;
> I'll bear the cross, endure the pain,
>   Supported by Thy Word.
>
> Thy saints, in all this glorious war,
>   Shall conquer, though they die;
> They view the triumph from afar,
>   And seize it with their eye.
>
> When that illustrious day shall rise,
>   And all Thy armies shine
> In robes of victory through the skies,
>   The glory shall be thine. Amen.[65]

Seemingly timeless, some hymns use war in a metaphorical sense to explain daily trials of the Christian experience; other hymns, however,, that make specific reference to actual warfare tend to grow from real situations. Yet, underlying, these "war" hymns is a deep desire for peace, making Charles C. Washburn's observation appropriate. "If there is one universal prayer in the hearts of men," says Washburn, "both in nations

that acknowledge God and among peoples who do not, it must

surely be that peace may prevail among all nations and peoples

of the earth."[66]

Echoing the ideals of peace and freedom, some American

hymns, like English hymns, grew out of the American Civil War

(1861-1865). This situation reinforces the idea that the hymn

can be a vehicle for man's desires and hopes, even if those

desires and hopes are merely political and not spiritual. For

example, contemplating the dilemma of the American nation,

James Russell Lowell penned this majestic hymn:

> Once to ev'ry man and nation
> Comes the moment to decide,
> In the strife of truth with falsehood,
> For the good or evil side;
> Some great cause, God's new Messiah,
> Off'ring each the bloom and blight,
> And the choice goes by forever
> 'Twixt that darkness and that light.
>
> Then to side with truth is noble,
> When we share her wretched crust
> Ere her cause bring fame and profit
> And 'tis prosperous to be just;
> Then it is the brave man chooses,
> While the coward stands aside
> Till the multitude make virtue
> Of the faith they had denied.
>
> By the light of burning martyrs
> Jesus' bleeding feet I track,
> Toiling up new Calvaries ever
> With the cross that turns not back;
> New occasions teach new duties,
> Time makes ancient good uncouth;
> They must upward still and onward
> Who would keep abreast of truth.
>
> Though the cause of evil prosper,

> Yet 'tis truth alone is strong,
> Though her portion be the scaffold,
> And upon the throne be wrong,
> Yet the scaffold sways the future,
> And behind the dim unknown
> Standeth God behind the shadow
> Keeping watch above his own.[67]

Powerful in every phrase, this unusual hymn discloses a
mind that is firmly set upon its perception of truth. The
opening lines are spurious because the choice between good and
evil is not given to men and nations only once, but rather, it
is given constantly. The hymn, however, remains intact because
in its majesty, it supports one of the fundamental principles
of democracy, the right of a man to choose. In its unwavering
conviction, furthermore, it supports truth, one of the
cornerstones of Christian life. In this instance, the hymn
becomes a manifesto of Christian virtues. Though not a
seventeenth-century hymn, it sprang from civil circumstances
similar to those of seventeenth-century England when men fought
and died for what they perceived to be religious truth and
religious freedom.

Defying the conventions of hymn writing, Lowell wrote his
hymn in a partially prosaic style. Its meter does not fit
either the common, the short nor the long meters usually used
in hymns,[6] and the eight-line stanza created a new rhyming
pattern. The first four lines conform to the a, b, c, b
pattern of the common meter, but the additional four lines,
though repetitive of the a, b, c, b cannot be thus designed;

hence, the stanzas rhyme a, b, c, b, d, e, f, e, a pattern very
uncommon in hymnody.

David Poling, discussing the importance of hymns throughout
the ages, points out that hymns are essential "for believing
peoples," for a new hymn "meant new information and reminders
of past victories."[69] Although Poling's statement may be aptly
applied to the seventeenth-century political hymn, one may
extend such a statement to assert that a new hymn sometimes
brings old virtues to the forefront. Indeed, Lowell's hymn
states that "new occasions teach new duties"; but the duties
are determined by old standards of truth.

In examining the themes of war peace and politics that
pervade the seventeenth-century hymn, one is forced to recall
the words of a previously cited authority, Frederick Gillman,
who posits that a hymn book is a "transcript from real life."[70]
Inasmuch as this statement applies to the present discussion,
it has relevance and credibility, because the seventeenth-
century hymn grew from ideological warfare, a circumstance of
real life. Furthermore, continually being waged, then, were
real wars that were serious demonstrations of verbal,
political, and religious battles. The seventeenth-century hymn
employs the imagery of war and peace to demonstrate the
internal strife and rest of the human spirit. Often, it makes
God a warrior and expresses the hope that Christian strivings
will cease and that peace will reign at last.

NOTES FOR CHAPTER IV

[1]John R. Greene, A Short History of the English People, Volume 3: 1603-1683 (New York: Nottingham Society, n.d.), pp. 295-296.

[2]Thomas Carlyle, ed., The Letters and Speeches of Oliver Cromwell (New York: AMS Press, 1945), p. 160.

[3]Percy Dearmer, The Story of the Prayer Book, pp. 97-98.

[4]Dearmer, "The Puritans in Power." Story of the Prayer Book, p. 99.

[5]Routley, Hymns and Human Life, pp. 59-60.

[6]Bratt, Rise and Development of Calvinism, p. 27 and Walzer, The Revolution of the Saints, p. 60.

[7]Schmidt, Calvin, pp. 122-123.

[8]John R. Green, Short History of the English People (London: 1897), ch. viii, stn. 5.

[9]See Phineas Fletcher's "Drop, drop slow tears,: English Hymnal, 89; Richard Baxter's "Ye Holy Angels Bright," Clarendon Hymn Book, 298; John Byrom's "My Spirit longs for thee," Clarendon Hymn Book, 233; Francis Quarles' "Thou are my Life," Clarendon Hymn Book, 284; Thomas Ken's "Glory to thee, in light arrayed," Oxford Hymn Book, 18; Tate and Brady, "To bless thy chosen race," Oxford Hymn Book, 314.

[10]Benjamin Brawley, The History of the English Hymn, p. 58.

[11]M. Francois Guizot, History of Oliver Cromwell and the English Commonwealth from the Execution of Cahrles I to the Death of Cromwell (Philadelphia: Blanchard and Lea, 1854), pp. 142-143.

[12]Carlyle, Letters and Speeches of Oliver Cromwell, II, pp. 206-216.

[13]Millar Patrick, The Supplement to the Handbook to the Chruch Hymnary (London: Oxford University Press, 1935), p. 51.

[14]A Jacobite was a partisan of the Stuarts after the Revolution of 1688. The term was derived from the Latin word for James, Jacobus.

138

[15]Sir Paul Harvey, ed. <u>The Oxford Companion to English Literature</u> 4th ed. (Oxford: Oxford University Press, 1967), p. 572.

[16]Julian, <u>Dictionary of Hymnology</u>, pp. 347-349.

[17]Arthur Pollard, <u>English Hymns</u> (London: Longman, Green and Co., 1960), p. 18.

[18]Charles Richards, <u>Songs of Christian Praise</u> (New York: Taintor Brothers, Merrill and Co., 1880), p. 65.

[19]<u>The Church Hymnal</u>, No. 417.

[20]Frank B. Merryweather, <u>The Evolution of the Hymn</u> (London: William Clowes & Sons Ltd., 1966), p. 11.

[21]Gillman, <u>Evolution of the English Hymn</u>, pp. 160-161.

[22]George Wither, "The Scholar's Purgatory" (London, 1624), n.p.

[23]Benson, <u>The English Hymn</u>, p. 66.

[24]Gillman, <u>Evolution of the English Hymn</u>, p. 161.

[25]Benson, <u>The English Hymn</u>, p. 65.

[26]George Wither, <u>Hymnes and Songs of the Church</u> London: 1623 (inscription).

[27]Julian, <u>Dictionary of Hymnology</u>, p. 347.

[28]Wither, <u>Hymnes and Songs</u>, pp. 213-214.

[29]Wither, <u>Hymes and Songs</u>, No. 87.

[30]Cicely V. Wedgewood, <u>Poetry and Politics Under the Stuarts</u> (Cambridge: Cambridge University Press, 1960), pp. 73-74.

[31]George Wither, <u>Hymnes and Songs,</u> No. 90.

[32]See note on neoplatonism (Chapter VI).

[33]Wither, <u>Hymnes and Songs</u>, No. 87.

[34]John Milton, <u>The Poetical Works of John Milton to which is Prefixed a Biography of the Author by his Nephew, Edward Phillips</u> (New York: D. Appleton and Co., 1859), p. 20.

[35]Wedgewood, <u>Poetry and Politics under the Stuarts</u>, p. 119.

[36]John Milton, <u>Complete Poetry and Selected Prose</u>, ed. E. H. Visak (Glasgow: Glasgow University Press, 1964), pp. 729-730.

[37]John Milton, <u>Complete Poetry and Selected Prose</u>, Library ed. (New York: Random House, 1941), p. 84.

[38]See Appendix A for yet another example of Milton's opposition to papacy.

[39]Milton, <u>Complete Poetry and Selected Prose</u>, Library ed., p. 85.

[40]Milton, <u>Complete Poetry</u>, p. 85.

[41]Greene, <u>History of the English People</u>, p. 582.

[42]John Milton, <u>The Poetical Works of John Milton, III,</u> David Masson, ed. (London: Macmillan and Co., 1874(, p. 15.

[43]Milton, "Samson Agonistes", <u>Complete Poetical Works</u>, p. 364.

[44]<u>The Clarendon Hymn Book</u>, No. 232, and Vaughan's <u>Sacred Poems</u>, p. 70.

[45]F. J. Gillman, <u>The Evolution of the Hymn</u>, p. 169.

[46]Vaughan, <u>Sacred Poems</u>, pp. 204-205, and Palgrave's <u>Treasury of Sacred Song</u>, p. 87.

[47]<u>The Oxford Hymn Book</u>, No. 215.

[48]Louis Benson, "The Hymns of John Bunyan", <u>Papers of the Hymn Society of America</u>, I (New York: Hymn Society, 1930), p. 3.

[49]<u>The English Hymnal</u>, p. 528.

[50]Millar Patrick, <u>The Story of the Church's Song</u> (Richmond: Va.: John Knox Press, 1962), p. 120.

[51]Richard Baxter, <u>The Poetical Fragments with Sacred Hymns</u> (London: Printed for William Pickering), 1681.

[52]Richard Baxter, <u>The Cure of Church Divisions</u> ed. Francis Asbury (New York: Lane and Scott, 1849), pp. vi-vii.

140

[53]Baxter, Church Divisions, pp. 116-117.

[54]The Clarendon Hymn Book, No. 220.

[55]The Clarendon Hymn Book, No. 190.

[56]The Clarendon Hymn Book, No. 161.

[57]William Simonds, History of English Literature, p. 202.

[58]George Wither, Hymnes and Songs and George McDonald, England's Antiphon (London: McMillan & Co., 1874), p. 160.

[59]The Church Hymnary, No. 676 (Presbyterian) and The Hymnal of the Protestant Episcopal Church, No. 556.

[60]The Church Hymnary, No. 147 (Presbyterian).

[61]Watts, Psalms and Hymns and Spiritual Songs, pp. 135-136.

[62]The Engloish Psalter, Old Version (London: John Day, 1561) Ps. 68 and The Psalms of Davind in Meeter (London: 1650) Ps. 68.

[63]Carlyle, Letters and Speeches of Oliver Cromwell, p. 160.

[64]The Hymnal of the Protestant Episcopl Church, No. 550.

[65]The Church Hymnal, No. 550.

[66]Charles C. Wasburn, Hymn Interpretations (Nashville: Cokesbury Press, 1938), p. 106.

[67]The Hymnal of the Protestant Episcopal Church, No. 519.

[68]Common meter is four lines with 8:6:8:6 beats and a, b, a, b, or a, b, c, b rhyme. Short meter: 4 lines 6:6:86, abab, or a, b, c, b. Long meter: 4 lines: 8:8:8:*; a, b, a, b; a, b, c, b; a, b, b, a. From William Reynold's A Survey of Christian Hymnody, (New York: Holt, Rinehart and Winston, Inc., 1963), pp. xii-xiii.

[69]David Poling, Songs of Faith: Signs of Hope (Waco, Texas: Word Books, 1976), p. 12.

[70]Gillman, Evolution of the English Hymn, p. 30.

CHAPTER V

LIFE AND DEATH IN THE SEVENTEENTH-CENTURY
ENGLISH HYMN

Religious poetry of the seventeenth century, and hymns in
particular, had utilitarian value. They were functioning works
of art that served to inspire others, to rebuke them,
contradict them, to express personal religious or political
sentiments, and to represent the thoughts of some of their
authors. It must be remembered that although there were
disagreements and factionalism, most of the key writers of
hymns were pious and religious men, who, regardless of their
causes, held common theological bases in Christianity. Many of
the hymns studied have to be examined within the context of the
developments within the Church of England particularly under
the Stuart kings. At that time, it appears, the act of hymn-
writing and the nature of the devotional verses imply that
these were relatively safe avenues of self expression during
the times of political upheaval.

The rapid changes and developments in seventeenth century
England forced thinking people to meditation. The success of
the Reformation left them religious freedom still so new, that
vestigies of Roman Catholicism were mingled with protestantism
in the innocent stimulation of the meditative life. One of
the outstanding themes in many of the hymns of meditation is
the expression of the supplicants' humility, their devotion to

spiritual tears to prepare them for the end, not only the end
of their individual lives, but the end of time. So troubled
was the political scene of the seventeenth century that most
hymn-writers of that age seemed to believe that the last
Judgement was close and would change the course of time. They
prayed and prepared for that time that would ease their state
of political unrest.

Our hymn writer who expressed this idea urgently is John
Milton. One of his best hymns, based upon Psalms 82, 85, and
86 and written in 1648, is still in use today. "The Lord will
come and not be slow,"[1] makes full mention of the closeness in
time of the "Lord's coming. Beyond that, the hymn is a plea
for God to "judge the earth" and "to redress the wicked earth".
Then justice and truth, the writer believes, will flourish from
the earth. Milton's hymn reflects, too, his philosophical
belief that the earth can be a place of truth and justice if
man attempts to gain higher knowledge of his potential good and
his potential understanding that will accrue from the strict
study and contemplation of spiritual matters. John Milton,
ascribed to himself through his more secular writings the
prophetic role of the wise seer-poet who would speak with
divine inspiration of things to come. Therefore, the prophetic
tone of this hymn marks it as a typical seventeenth-century
piece, typical of Milton's thought and stance also expressed in
some of his secular pieces.[2]

The related idea of millenarianism is expressed by Tate and Brady whose familiarity with the Psalms through their work with the various editions of the Psalter of the Anglican church made it easy for them to base their hymns upon specific psalms. For instance, Psalm 130 inspired their hymn, "My soul with patience waits,"[3] in which the persona displays anxiety for the day of judgement. Whereas the psalm begins with a supplication and then mentions the power of God's forgiveness, the vigil of the righteous, and redemption; the hymn focuses mainly upon the waiting for the God of mercy.

Upon this principle of Christianity monastic groups were formed in England during the mid-seventeenth century when the concept of millenarianism became popular. Indeed, the small, religious community of Little Gidding founded by Nicholas Ferrar at Huntingdonshire became quite famous and exerted influence in the spiritual life of Anglicans. The community made up of members of Ferrar's family and close friends was based upon continuous devotions. Hourly services were held and sentinels took turns throughout the night to watch and pray, for they lived in daily anticipation of Christ's second coming. Tradition believes that George Herbert and Richard Crashaw were both influenced by the life of intense devotion at Little Gidding.

Graham Parry explains well the literature of tears related also to the kindred emotion of melancholy which was also

144

popular earlier in England. Parry posits that the cult of
tears emanated from the tears of Mary Magdalene[4] and inspired
other literature such as Richard Crashaw's poem, "The Weeper."
Parry writes:

> The cult of tears[was] encouraged by the
> Catholic Counter Reformation to direct the
> affections and emotions to a holy end: tears
> were the consequence of the faithful soul's
> infinite sorrow at the sufferings of Christ,
> and infinite joy at the miracle of salvation
> made possible by Christ's sacrifice. Because
> the tears sprang from a spiritual source,
> they were qualitatively superior to tears
> shed for human misfortunes and delights.
> Some devotional exercises incited weeping as
> a high emotional surrender to the great
> mysteries of faith; where the intellect could
> not longer proceed, feelings and intuitions
> advanced to a profounder understanding, and
> the visible expression of this state of faith
> was tears.[5]

Two major seventeenth-century hymn writers contributed to
preoccupation with the end of life in hymns that are still
popular in congregational singing today. Joseph Addison's
finely wrought hymn makes use of the Christian's "tears" as the
major manifestation of faith. Using rhetorical questions,
Addison develops the hymn to its climax in stanza 4 and
concludes it with certainty and assurance, qualities absent in
the introductory verses. The hymn reads:

> When rising from the bed of death,
> O'erwhelmed with guilt and fear,
> I see my Maker face to face,
> O how shall I appear?
>
> If yet, while pardon may be found,
> And mercy may be sought,
> My heart with inward horror shrinks,

And trembles at the thought;

When thou, O Lord, shall stand disclosed,
In majesty severe,
And sit in judgement on my soul,
O how shall I appear?

But thou hast told the troubled mind
Who does her sins lament,
The timely tribute of her tears
Shall endless woe prevent.

Then see the sorrow of my heart,
Ere yet it is too late;
And hear my savior's dying groans
To give those sorrows weight.

For never shall my soul despair
Her pardon to procure
Who knows thy only son has died
To make her pardon sure.

(<u>The English Hymnal</u>, no. 92)

Addison's hymn is complex, making use of the argumentative style, the balanced expression of "If . . . ., Then . . . .," promoting logic and reason, while at the same time injecting situational moment of death so that the total effect of the hymn is dramatic. Phineas Fletcher (1582-1659), on the other hand has produced a most effective hymn, still sung to a simple tune written by Orlando Gibbons (1583-1625). The beauty of this hymn is seen in its simplicity and in its well focused theme of tears. The hymn reads:

Drop, drop slow tears
And bathe those beauteous feat,
Which brought from heaven
The news and Prince of Peace.

Cease not, wet eyes,
His mercies to entreat;
To cry for vengeance

Sin doth never cease.

In your deep floods
Drown all my faults and fears
Nor let his eye
See sin but through my tears.

(The English Hymnal, no. 98)

The imagery of the tearful Christian is consistent throughout this hymn. There are no other major ideas detracting from the stark relief of the penitent sinner, a good example of the varying stylistic level that these early hymn writers achieved.

Samuel Crossman (1624-1683) the Dean of Bristol Cathedral focused on the idea of his own death as a time when he would leave all earthy cares behind. The emphasis is upon heaven as a "happy" place. Crossman writes:

Sweet place; sweet place alone!
The court of God most High,
The heaven of heavens, the throne
Of spotless majesty!
O happy place! when shall I be,
My God, with thee, to see thy face?[6]

To the seventeenth-century christian such as Crossman a state of dying was a moment of joy. This seventeenth century attitude to death is exemplified in the lives of some of the hymn writers. Bishop Thomas Ken, for example, was court chaplain of King Charles II, a well known hymn writer, and one of the seven bishops committed to prison because of refusal to acquiesce to the tyrant king, James II; also, later, Bishop Ken refused to take the Oath of Allegiance to William III. As

Bishop Ken grew older, he carried with him his shroud so "that he might be ready when the last messenger came."[7] In a similar fashion, almost, John Donne, who spent the second half of his life writing devotional poetry and preparing for death, demonstrated his preparedness by requesting a portrait of himself in his funeral dress. His biographer Isaac Walton, records the practice as follows:

> Several charcoal fires being first made in his large study, he brought with him into that place his winding-sheet in his hand, and having put off all his clothes had this sheet put upon him, and so tied with knots at his head and feet, and his hand so placed as dead bodies are usually fitted to be shrouded and put into their coffin, or grave. Upon this urn he thus stood, with his eyes shut, and with so much of the sheet turned aside as might show his lean, pale and death-like face, which was purposely turned towards the east from whence he expected the second coming of his and our Savior Jesus. In this posture he was drawn at his just height.[8]

Hymn writers, Joseph Stennett (1663-1713) and Thomas Shepherd (1665-1739) both spanning the centuries express the idea that the crosses of the earth, or the troubles of life are exchanged for the crown or kingly status in the after-life. The symbol of the crown signifying well-being is an interesting one in the hymns because it shows the belief that the heavenly kingdom was unlike the kingdoms that man had created. Earthly kingdoms were full or strife, but apparently the hymn writers envisioned the monarch's life as enviable. Both these excerpts from hymn writers illustrate the point. Shepherd writes:

> The consecrated cross I'll bear,
> Till death shall set me free,
> And then go home my crown to wear
> For there's a crown for me.
>
> O precious cross! O glorious crown!
> O resurrection day!
> Ye angels from the stars come down,
> And bear my soul away.[9]

Stennet emphasizes death as the end of pains:

> The heavenly claim within the breast
> Is the dear pledge of glorious rest
> Which for the church of God remains
> The end of cares, the end of pains.[10]

The gloom that shrouds so many of the earlier hymn writers of England was not an indication of personal sadness, but rather, an indication that they had surveyed the heights of religious thought and thus, "the weeping eye," akin to Christ's tears of love, is commonly seen. This need to live a life in preparation for the next is exemplified well by John Donne. Of him Graham Parry writes:

> Donne was disposed to believe that he was
> living in the last age of the world, a view
> widely shared by his protestant
> contemporaries . . . . Although Donne's
> religious poems served a private function of
> spiritual discipline . . . they also had a
> social function for he circulated them to
> friends so that they could serve the needs of
> others.[11]

Parry goes on to show, through Donne, one of the important aspects of the "cult of tears," the constant striving of man through prayer, meditation, and kind deeds to reach spiritual perfection and thus, gain, everlasting acceptance. Parry writes of Donne:

> The 'Hymne to God my God in my sickness' and
> 'A Hymne to God the Father' were exceptional
> productions... The first Hymne flourishes
> his wit and learning; the second is unusually
> simple and direct, but still manages a witty
> appeal for the forgiveness of sins. Both
> poems illustrate the Art of Dying as it was
> practiced in the early seventeenth century.
> A self-conscious pose on one's deathbed was
> considered admirable, because a well-
> sustained performance edified the spectators
> who themselves would eventually have to play
> the part, and also allowed the dying person
> to compose his soul, extemporize appropriate
> Christian prayers and make an exemplary
> Christian end.[12]

Logically, the expectation of death, the last day, and a

judgement provided the seventeenth century Christians with a

defined opportunity to prepare their souls. Louis Martz

discusses this problem in considering that age and he points to

a French publication that focuses on self analysis as the major

weapon in spiritual combat. The Christian Pilgrime in his

Spiritualle Conflict and Conquest, was published in Paris in

1652. Martz suggests that this two part work may have held

significance for English Literature of the seventeenth century

since it proposed that self analysis is "dramatically related

to the universal order of things ... the spiritual life

consists of ... knowing the infinite greatness and goodness of

God, together with a true sense of our own weakness and

tendency to evil."[13]

A general religious belief of the age seen in hymns as well

as other literary works is that singularly, the "vicious

tendencies of man must be attacked and diminished in power."

150

The _Combat_ urged Christians to attack vices systematically and
incessantly:

> The first thing to do when you awake is to
> open the windows of your soul. Consider
> yourself as on the field of battle and facing
> the enemy ... either fight or die.
>   Imagine the enemy before you, that
> particular vice or disorderly passion that
> you are trying to conquer. . . . At the same
> time, picture at your right Jesus Christ your
> Invincible Leader, accompanied by the Blessed
> Virgin, St. Joseph, whole companies of angels
> and saints, and particularly by the glorious
> Archangel Michael. At your left is Lucifer
> and his troops, ready to support the passion
> or vice you are fighting . . .
>   Begin to fight immediately in the name of
> the Lord, armed with distrust in yourself
> with confidence in God, [with] prayer, and
> with correct use of the faculties of your
> soul.[14]

Such was the conviction of many seventeenth century
protestants who rejected the idea of man as an intermediary to
God, of pardon purchased through confession and atonement. The
Christian's occupation and preoccupation was to secure eternal
peace and pardon by self analysis, self control, discipline and
contemplation of the Scriptures. The hymns of Isaac Watts
abound with examples of the Christian, protestant principles of
the day, but these verses of hymns set forth below demonstrate
the soul in readiness for death. This attitude towards death,
Judgement Day, and Redemption is a desired state, after man has
"made" himself ready by spiritual "combat" against passion and
other temptations using the weapons of communion, "distrust in
self, confidence in God, 'exercise'--that is the proper use of

the senses and the faculties of the soul in considerations
directed toward the extricating of vices and the planting of
virtues--and prayer, which includes both petition and
meditation.[15]

Built upon particular selections from the Scriptures,
Watts's hymns speak for themselves:

> Jesus the vision of thy face
> Hath overpowering charms!
> Scarce shall I feel death's cold embrace
> If Christ be in my arms.
>
> Then while ye hear my heart-strings break
> How sweet my minutes roll!
> A mortal paleness on my cheek
> And glory in my soul.
>
> (Taken from Psalms and Hymns, no. 19, "Lord,
>   at thy temple we appear," based upon
>   Luke II, 27)

Hymn no. 61, "Now to the Lord, that makes us know" is based
upon Revelation I, verses 5 through 7 which mention the wailing
that the world will do at the Second Coming:

> The unbelieving world shall wail
> While we rejoice to see the day;
> Come, Lord, nor let thy promise fail
> Nor let thy chariot long delay

This hymn indicates that it is only the unbelieving that will
be in distress at the Second Coming; it suggests that the
believers, having "wailed" throughout life will be in a state
of rejoicing. The hymn below, quoted in its entirety, best
exemplifies the assurance of the believer:

> There is a house not made with hands,
> Eternal and on high;
> And there my spirit waiting stands,

Till God shall bid it fly.

Shortly this prison of my clay
Must be dissolved and fall;
Then, O my soul, with joy obey
Thy heavenly Father's call.

Tis he, by his almighty grace
That forms thee fit for heaven
And, as an earnest of the place
Hath his own spirit given.

We walk by faith of joys to come;
Faith lives upon his word
But while the body is our home
We're absent from the Lord.

'Tis pleasant to believe they grace
But we had rather see;
We would be absent from the flesh,
And present, Lord, with thee.

(Hymn no. 110, based upon
  2 Corinthians V, 1, 5, 8)

These types of hymns were of extreme utilitarian value in congregational singing. Keyed to specific texts, the preachers could unify texts of Scriptures, sermons, and hymns. Hence, for a given service, the congregation was emersed in a particular theme, bombarded as it were with repetitive messages, through the senses as well as the mind. If the sermon were missed, then the scripture reading, or the hymn would suffice.

Additionally, as was stated before, literal interpretation of the Scriptures allowed for little use of the imagination, free will, or alternative thought of any kind. Therefore, the term "believer" was a serious word that denoted readiness in spiritual matters, and connotated an unreadiness to accommodate much else that was developing during the seventeenth century.

In this respect, and with this focus on "the end", the seventeenth century hymn is unlike some literature of its age for knowledge was exploding in England and around the world, in general, and men like Browne, and Bacon were concerned with the place of science and discovery in religion. For them, the age was a beginning, not an end. They thought, "we are not accustomed in modern books of science to an unobtrusive irony which can make jokes with quiet solemnity and touch religious mysteries with a reverent smile."[16] Thomas Browne, concerned with the inseparable problem of religion and science said, "We shall not, I hope, disparage the Resurrection of our Redeemer, if we say the Sun doth not dance on Easter Day[17]

Whereas most of the hymn writers, in general were looking to the past, the ancients; a few seventeenth century writers such as Milton and Bacon were broader in their approach and Douglas Bush reconciles these contrary directions by the following line of thought:

> In the quarrel of the ancients and moderns,
> science, especially applied science, led the
> van of modernism and progress. Bacon even
> minimized the difficulties of his own
> induction in his earnest efforts to banish
> despair and all the other obstacles which
> stood between man and the conquest of nature,
> and his message owed something of its
> emotional force to his sense of man's actual
> misery as well as of his potential grandeur .
> . . . The present and not the classical past
> is the ripe maturity of the race. Bacon,
> Browne, and Milton, in their several ways,
> are expressly seeking to repair the ruins of

Adam, to restore man's forfeited heritage.[18]

The scientists and philosophers that Bush mentions accept
man's heritage as the future. Technically, they are similar to
the hymn writers discussed in this chapter. The divergence of
thought occurs in the concept that each group holds of the
future. Whereas the hymn writers prepared for their future
through prayer, waiting, tears, and joy, and celebrated the
promise, salvation and heaven, the philosophers and scientists
of the age celebrated God's gift of life and earth the future,
the unknown. This divergence is typical of the seventeenth
century, and each group, without being conscious of its
contribution shaped in an unmistakable manner the future of
their culture.

[1]The Hymnal of the Protestant Episcopal Church (1940) no. 312.

[2]See Milton's "Ode on the Morning of Christ's Nativity" and his poem on "The Passion."

[3]The Hymnal of the Protestant Episcopal Church (1940) no. 439.

[4]Graham Parry, Seventeenth-Century Poetry: The Social Context (London: Hutchinson and Co. (Publishers Ltd. 1985) p. 131.

[5]Parry, pp. 131-132.

[6]Edward S. Ninde, Nineteen Centuries of Christian Song, (New York: Fleming H. Revell Company 1938) p. 87.

[7]Ninde, pp. 90-92.

[8]Izaac Walton, 'The Life of Dr. Donne' in Walton's Lives ed. C. H. Dick (London, n.d.) p. 57.

[9]The Church Hymnary Edwin A. Bedell, comp., (New York: Merrill and Co. 1893) no. 571.

[10]The Church Hymnary, no. 34.

[11]Parry, pp. 67-68.

[12]Parry, p. 69.

[13]See Louis L. Martz's, The Poetry of Meditation (New Haven: Yale Univ. Press 1954) pp. 126-127.

[14]See Martz, p. 126.

[15]See Martz, p. 127.

[16]Douglas Bush, English Literature in the Earlier Seventeenth Century (Oxford: Clarendon Press, 1964) p. 274.

[17]Bush, p. 274.

[18]Bush, p. 274.

CHAPTER VI

SECULAR CONCERNS
THE SEVENTEENTH CENTURY ENGLISH HYMN

Upon reading some seventeenth-century hymns, one is tempted to label as humor what was, then, at the time of composition, a genuine allusion to seventeenth-century life. These allusions, images, or references, in some instances, provide insight into the secular concerns of the age. In this respect, the seventeenth-century hymn is much like the rest of seventeenth-century literature.

Often regarded as a century of drastic transition, the seventeenth century marks the decline of the absolute authority of ancient views and ushered in the birth of a scientific and experimental era. Within a half century, scientific thought made substantial progress in laying the foundation for modern concepts.

Practical astronomy had progressed in the late sixteenth century through the work of Tycho Bache (1546-1601), but the publication De Magnete (1600) of William Gilbert set in motion a chain of major scientific discoveries that typify scientific progress of the seventeenth century. For example, Kepler (1571-1630)[1] developed the orbital laws of the universe, and this development enhanced the Copernican or Heliocentric Theory that the universe is sun-centered, thus disproving the old Ptolemaic Theory that the earth was the center of the universe.

In the fields of astronomy and mathematics, discoveries

were made in several countries which changed the entire world
and had direct impact upon life and thought in England. Travel
became easier, and man's knowledge of the physical world
increased but was slowly accepted. Galileo (1564-1642)
invented the telescope and refined the Copernican Theory, but
he remained a religious man. He was, at times, engaged in
justifying the Bible. An interesting episode from his life
serves to illustrate the conflict between religion and science
during that age. Galileo argued before the Roman Inquisition
that only the Copernican Theory could make possible Joshua's
command for the sun to stand still.[2] In the Ptolemaic System,
out of logical necessity, Joshua would have to command all
other planets to stand still in order to prevent orbital
collision. Also, in a letter to Father Costelli, Professor of
mathematics at Pisa, Galileo in 1613 explains his belief in the
Scriptures and his skepticism toward the interpreters thereof:

> It seems to me that it is well said . . .
> that the Holy Scriptures cannot err, and that
> decrees therein contained are absolutely true
> and inviolable . . . but though Scripture
> cannot err, its expounders and interpreters
> are liable to err in many ways . . . Holy
> Scripture and nature are both emanations from
> the Divine word: the former dictated by the
> Holy Writ, the latter the executrix of God's
> commands.[3]

Here, Galileo insists that Scriptures teach those things
"necessary to salvation," but he admits its insufficiency since
it does not teach that which one may learn from his senses and
his intelligence that are also gifts from God.

Although Galileo and other seventeenth-century scientists remained devout men while they concentrated on scientific development, their work was viewed with mixed feelings by skeptics as well as converts, and the church could not tolerate any philosophy which tampered with accepted Biblical truths. The result is partially reflected in the various attitudes toward science seen in some seventeenth-century hymns.

Among other scientific work which affected seventeenth-century thought are Dr. William Harvey's discovery of the system of blood circulation, Sir Isaac Newton's discovery of mathematical principles, Francis Bacon's attempt at scientific methods, and Descartes' "Theory of the Vortices."[4]

With convincing regularity, the theme of transition haunts the English hymn of the seventeenth century. Appearing in John Quarles' hymn, "Long did I toil," the stanza below not only mentions change but also reflects the contemporary scientific interests:

> What e'er may change, in Him no change is seen,
> O glorious sun that wanes not nor declines,
> Above the clouds and storms he walks serene,
> And on his people's inward darkness shines
> All may depart, I fret not nor repine,
> While I my Savior's am, while He is mine.[5]

While finding solace in the constancy of God, this hymn writer notes that all else is subject to mutability. The hymn draws a subtle comparison between the Son of God and the sun, since neither "wanes nor declines." Reflecting the current scientific interest in the Heliocentric Theory, the hymn

utilizes to the fullest extent the metaphor of the sun. John
Quarles returns to this theme in yet another hymn, "Fountain of
light and living breath." In Stanza IV, he writes of earthly
changes:

> When winter fortunes cloud the brows
> Of summer friends, when eyes grow strange,
> When plighted faith forgets its vows,
> When earth and all things in it change,
> O Lord, thy mercies fail me never,
> When one thou lov'st, thou lov'st forever.[6]

Although Quarles' central argument is the unfailing,
merciful constancy of God, he uses the fickle nature of man as
a foil to his major point and, in doing so, refers to
circumstances that reflect many of the social concerns of the
seventeenth century. For instance, elsewhere in this work, it
is demonstrated that because of religious or political
differences, friends could easily become enemies; also, because
of political persuasion, men at times changed their faith and
forgot their vows. Additionally, scientific thought was
changing the world and much that was in it. Quarles's hymn
quoted above may be viewed, therefore, as a personal reaction
to the forces of transition in seventeenth-century life.

Writing of seventeenth-century secular concerns, Henry King
and Phineas Fletcher, two hymn writers of that age produced
similar hymns. Both hymns, parallel in several respects,
mention the sun, a seemingly public reference in the
seventeenth century. Henry King, Bishop of Chichester, one of
the Cambridge Platonists, writes with constant reference to

seventeenth-century everyday activities.

> Except the Lord the house sustain,
> The builder's labor is in vain;
> Except the city he defend,
> And to the dwellers safety send
> In vain are sentinels prepared,
> Or armed watchmen for the guard.

> You vainly with the earthly light
> Arise, or sit up late at night
> To find support and daily eat
> Your bread with sorrow earned and sweat;
> When God who his beloved keeps
> This plenty gives with quiet sleeps.[7]

Equally laden with secular references to the builder and the fortresses in Phineas Fletcher's hymn:

> If God build not the house, and lay
> The groundwork sure - whoever build
> It cannot stand one stormy day.
> If God be not the city's shield,
> If He be not their bars and wall,
> In vain is watchtower men and all.

> Though then thou wak'st when others rest,
> Thou rising thou prevents't the sun
> Though with vain care thou daily feast
> Thy labours lost, and thou undone;
> But God his child will feed and keep
> And draw the curtains to his sleep.[8]

Using imagery and symbols familiar to them and popular during their age, both hymn writers deal with the theme of divine protection. Arguing that no foundation devoid of God will last, these hymns are based upon the first verse of Psalm CXXVII that states:

> Except the Lord build the house, they
> Labor in vain that build it: except the
> Lord keep the city, the watchmen waketh but
> in vain.

As seventeenth-century leaders arose and vanished so too did their policies and their laws. The truism of this passage could, therefore, be applied to either the Puritan or Royalist forces in seventeenth-century political and religious life. Each faction claimed that the other's foundation is not of God and, therefore, can not survive. Adapting the passage for its relevance, both hymn writers inject the idea of armed sentinels common to the Royalist faction.

Viewing the transitional phase somewhat differently, Thomas Campion (1567-1620), a well known Elizabethan secular song writer with few hymns to his credit, refers to the confusion of the age, for admittedly there was confusion in seventeenth-century life. He writes of old and new beliefs:

> Farewell, World, thou mass of mere confusion,
> False light with many shadows dimn'd,
> Old witch, with new foils trimm'd
> Thou deadly sleep of soul, and charm'd illusion.[9]

Mentioning the falsity of the age, possibly civil falsity, Campion turns to the metaphor of the witch, and the superstition of the nocturnal activities of magicians, a relic of medieval days. Pagan ideas in coexistence with Christian idea, evidenced in this hymn, also appear in the wider body of seventeenth-century literary works such as Robert Herrick's poems. Such works show that transition, in the seventeenth century, was not sudden , but was rather "like the transition of the seasons,"[10] as Edgar Newgrass observed. Just as hymns were in existence side-by-side with metrical psalms, so, too, old ideas lingered alongside the new. The idea of seventeenth-century transition is best summarized by Alexander

Judson's observation:

> Vastly interesting spiritual changes
> occurred; . . . men began the century as
> children, still possessing much of the
> bouyancy and glow of Elizabethan England,
> then ended it men and women, with the more
> sobered and thoughtful modern outlook. In no
> other hundred years has the English race
> undergone a more profound mental change.[11]

Perhaps the most popular hymn exemplifying the conflicting

ideas of the age is George Herbert's hymn "Teach me my God and

King," which is an adaptation of his poem "The Elixer":

> Teach me my God and King
> In all things thee to see;
> And what I do in anything,
> To do it as for thee.
>
> All may of Thee partake,
> Nothing can be so mean
> Which with this tincture, "for thy sake"
> Will not grow bright and clean.
>
> A servant with this cause
> Makes drudgery divine,
> Who sweeps a room, as for thy laws
> Makes that and the action fine.
>
> This is the famous stone
> That turneth all to gold;
> For that which God doth touch and own
> Cannot for less be told. Amen[12]

A careful interpretation of this hymn reveals Herbert's

concern with secular matters. In the opening stanza, the poet

asks God to help him see Him in all things, that is to say, God

in everything, a theological adaptation of Platonism.[13]

Continuing, the poet links to the first a second request that

whatever he does be done in God's name. The poet, being the

doer, the request becomes an assertion that he will do anything or everything in God's name. In Stanza II, the hymn writer asserts that all things (or persons) may partake of God. He uses a powerful chemical reference to a tincture, a tint or substance applied to another to produce a color and pervasive effect. The last line of Stanza II concludes the chemical metaphor that this tincture will produce a bright, clear, clean color when used for God's sake. In doing God's work and using the "tincture" of God's cause, His servant changes mere drudgery into something divine.

Intensifying the chemical image, Herbert adds one from alchemy, a pseudo-science still held in some esteem in Herbert's day when chemistry was rapidly replacing alchemy: drudgery will become divine when God's love becomes the cause of refining agent. An effective metaphysical image closes the hymn: sweeping a room becomes a lofty act, if the scientific laws, are in operation as they would be in a chemical laboratory. The poet assures the critical analyst of his meaning by stating in the last stanza that the famous philosopher's stone, the elixir, in this instance, is God's love that transmutes all things to gold and, therefore, cannot be valued for less. In these scientific references, the hymn writer has demonstrated an intense secular concern. Ben Jonson's famous play The Alchemist is based on a similar theme, that of pretending by means of alchemy to change baser metals into gold.

Herbert's use of popular beliefs, however, makes the hymn understandable to the people of his day. Additionally, the entire hymn assumes a deeper meaning upon the examination of Herbert's devotion to music. Participating in private weekly music meetings was one of Herbert's pleasures. For these meetings, he composed poems and set them to music, and to these meetings all his friends and neighbors were invited to participate along with his entire household.[14] This hymn, "The Elixer," suggests the democratic, egalitarian spirit, an interpretation in keeping with the foregoing, and should be interpreted, moreover, to mean that God's service and one's participating in his love is the "famous stone" that refines man's base nature.

The original composition of "The Elixer" contained the following stanzas:

> Not rudely, as a beast
> To runne into an action;
> But still to make the prepossest,
> And give it his perfection.
>
> A man that looks on glasse
> On it may stay his eye,
> Or if he pleaseth, though it passe
> And then the heav'n espy.[15]

Evidenced in the first stanza here is an anthropological thought that man is not like a beast that acts upon instinct, but that man has reason. This though which gained popularity during the eighteenth century, the Age of reason, was in its nascence here. This interest in man and his behavior may be interpreted as the forerunner of modern behavioral psychology. More important, however, are the last two lines of the first stanza. The poet states that man's responsibility is to "make" that in him which is "prepossessed" and to give that prepossession "his perfection." Embedded here is the deist idea that man is born with some innate or inner qualities, possibly spiritual qualities (God in everything) and that it is man's duty to "make" or tend these qualities to their perfection, a philosophy suggesting the possibility of the perfectibility of man, a timeless subject of intellectual debate.

Making reference to yet another branch of science, astronomy, which made great gains during the seventeenth century, Herbert compares the Christian to the astronomer who may simply choose to gaze on the eye-piece of his telescope or to gaze through it to the heavens. Although the eye-piecer is merely convex lens, one may observe the infinite realms above the earth if one chooses to look beyond its one dimension. In short, one may catch a glimpse of another world. Musings such as these probably prompted Homer Rodheaver to state that "The Elixir" is meditative rather than hymnic in character,[16] but these two qualities have peacefully co-existed in this excellent hymn of Herbert's creation.

On the contrary, in the stanzas of the Reverend Robert

Herrick (1591-1674), one finds a tone more frivolous than
Herbert's, as well as a subject matter less profound than
Herbert's; yet, it is also representative of seventeenth-
century thought, and provides instances to illustrate the
secular concerns of the age. Robert Herrick is best known as
a Cavalier poet. Usually the Cavaliers were Royalists who
generally wrote poetry on worldly matters. According to Harvey
B. Marks, "not even the gayest of Cavaliers failed to write
some sacred verse or prayer of aspiration during the Puritan
interlude."[17] In keeping with the trends of the age, Herrick,
in 1648, published Noble Numbers, a volume of sacred poems.
Simonds states that "there is no indication in his [Herrick's]
writings that he was moved by the momentous events of the days
in which he lived. There is much of the joy of mere living."[18]
Herrick's attitude is enlightening to the scholar of
seventeenth-century thought, for one may conclude that as
"momentous" and stormy as times were then, there were those who
were able to extricate themselves from the political and
religious struggles long enough to write of the joys of living.
To dismiss Herrick's work because it fails to reflect the
"momentous" seventeenth century would be a mistake, for while
Herbert indirectly recorded the philosophy of the age, and
Donne and Watts the theology, Herrick recorded some of the
everyday activities, and, thus, contributed to the concept of
the concern of the seventeenth century for secular along with

sacred matters. Herrick's "Litany to the Holy Spirit" is his

best contribution through hymnody to this concern. In the

English Hymnal the modern version reads:

> In the hour of my distress
> When temptations me oppress
> And when I my sins confess
> Sweet Spirit, comfort me.
>
> When I lie within my bed
> Sick in heart and sick in head,
> And with doubts discomforted
> Sweet spirit, comfort me.
>
> And when judgement is revealed,
> And that opened which was sealed,
> And to theee I have appealed,
> Sweet spirit, comfort me.[19]

Included in the original version of this hymn, however, are

these and other stanzas as well, more typical of the secular

concerns of the seventeenth century:

> When the artless doctor sees
> Not one hope but of his fees,
> And his skill runs on the less
> Sweet Spirit, comfort me.
>
> When his potion and his pill
> Is of none or little skill
> Meet for nothing but to kill
> Sweet spirit, comfort me.
>
> When the passing bell doth toll
> And the furies in a shoal
> Come to fright a passing soul
> Sweet spirit, comfort me.[20]

In the original version, the poet displays interest in the

secular view of the physician. He is not a scientific figure

with knowledge but, rather, an artist with skill. Displaying

his knowledge of the Hippocratic oath to which doctors

subscribed in his day, the hymn writer reveals his interest in a secular matter. Although the seventeenth-century view of the doctor and his fees may have survived to contemporary times, the idea of medicine as an art is somewhat outdated.

Another contemporary reference in this version, moreover, is the reference to furies "come to fright a passing soul." Belief in the powers of darkness, witchcraft, furies and the like was widespread in Herrick's day as James I's book on Daemonology, Shakespeare's <u>Macbeth</u>, and other writings attest. This is an illustration, moreover, of a pagan thought surviving alongside a Christian one. The concept, nevertheless, is seen in other English writings of that time. The idea of furies frightening the passing soul also appears at the climax of <u>Doctor Faustus</u>, Christopher Marlowe's famous Elizabethan play. At Faustus' moment of death, devils appear and Faustus exclaims:

> My God, My God, look not so fiercely on me!
> Adders and serpents, let me breathe a while!
> Ugly hell, gape not! Come not, Lucifer!
> (V.iii. 185-187)

Thomas Campion (1567-1620),[21] a lyrical poet, also uses this general type of imagery in certain stanzas of the hymns, "Straight the caves of hell" and "The man of life upright," quoted below:

> The man of life upright
> Whose guiltless heart is free
> From all dishonest deeds,
> Or thought of vanity;

The man whose silent days
In harmless joys are spent,
Whom hopes cannot delude,
Nor sorrow discontent.

That man needs neither towers
Nor armor for defense,
Nor secret vaults to fly
From thunder's violence.

He only can behold
With unaffrighted eyes
The horrors of the deep
And terrors of the skies.

Thus, scorning all the cares
That fate or fortune brings,
He makes the heaven his book
His wisdom, heavenly things.

Good thoughts his only friends,
His wealth a well-spent age,
The earth his sober inn
And quiet pilgrimage.[22]

This hymn is not in current use, but it is important for its
ideas on secular as well as sacred matters. Germane to this
discussion of secular concerns of the seventeenth-century hymns
is Campion's awareness of "dishonest deeds," "vanity,"
"Harmless joys," "secret vaults," "cares" and "fortune." All
these worldly concerns had become a part of the new economic
development of seventeenth-century England. Campion's song on
the other hand, supports the upright honest life and it
promises peace of mind to those who adopt that way of life.
Furthermore, death is viewed as a "pilgrimage." The song
promises that the honest man need not be afraid at the hour of
death; instead, he will enter the "earth, his sober inn/and
quiet pilgrimage." Although these ideas are simple, they carry

great meaning, for the words "inn" and "pilgrimage" are
contrary. Through use of contradictory terms, Campion infuses
the idea of a burial as being merely the first or the
preparatory stage of the journey which man's soul makes.
Embedded in the hymn, therefore, is a metaphysical concept
alongside the more ordinary materialistic and moralistic
concepts of the age. This duality helps to explain the
references to the troubled souls who see "fiends" coming to
escort them at the hour of death as is illustrated in Campion's
hymn quoted below:

> Straight the caves of Hell
> Dressed with flowers I see,
> Wherein False pleasures dwell
> That winning most, most deadly be.
>
> Throngs of mask'd fiends
> Wing'd like angels fly,
> E'en the gates of friends
> In fair disguise black dangers lie.[23]

Once more, the hymns exhibit similarities with the
standard, accepted body of seventeenth century literature.
Traces of science mingle with mythology, and Christian thoughts
are interspersed with pagan ones. All combine to reflect many
of the popular secular concerns of the age. These hymns also
serve to reinforce Herbert Jefferson's standard and method of
evaluating hymns. He suggests that one sound method to employ
in discerning the quality of a hymn is to "abstract single
lines and podner their significance." He goes on to suggest
that often, a hymn which appears at first to be simplistic may

by this analysis yield "treasures of thought and vision beyond expectation, if it is truly a hymn of merit."[24]

Interest in Thomas Campion's work extends beyond the theme of his hymns to the fact that some of them were actually passed on in their original setting and, today, still show their appropriateness. For instance, his hymn "View me, O Lord, a work of thine" was set to the music of Orlando Gibbons (1583-1625) and this hymn, has survived through three centuries because of its statement. The hymn writer asks God to view him as a divine creation, again a reference to the neo-platonic ideas of the age.

Continuing into the seventeenth century from the Elizabethan Age was the notion that man's knowledge could be significantly increased through travel. The adventurous spirit of the Renaissance still survived, and writers such as Sir Walter Raleigh and Richard Hakluyt popularized the travelogue in their respective works, Divers Voyages Touching upon the Discoveries of America (1582) and The Principall Navigations. In the travelogues the writers expressed a desire to see new worlds, a lust to accumulate gold, and a hope to add, through conquest, protestant nations to Britain's dominions.

With this surge in geographical activity, substantial impact was made upon the seventeenth-century hymn. One may even postulate that the imperialism that triumphed in the well-known hymn of Kipling had its beginnings in the seventeenth-

century hymn. For instance, Kipling's "Recessional," a hymn of
great dignity and stature in the hierarchy of English hymns,
reads as follows:

> God our Fathers, known of old,
> Lord of our far-flung battle line,
> Beneath whose awful hand we hold
> Dominion over palm and pine --
> Lord God of Hosts be with us yet,
> Lest we forget -- lest we forget!
>
> The tumult and the shouting dies,
> The captains and the Kings depart;
> Still stands thine ancient sacrifice,
> An humble and a contrite heart.
> Lord God of hosts be with us yet,
> Lest we forget -- lest we forget!
>
> Far-called our navies melt away;
> On dune and headland sinks the fire:
> Lo, all our pomp of yesterday
> Is one with Nineveh and Tyre!
> Judge of the nations, spare us yet
> Lest we forget -- lest we forget!
> If, drunk with sight of power, we lose
> Wild tongues that have not thee in awe,
> Such boastings as the Gentiles use,
> Or lesser breeds without the law --
> Lord God of hosts be with us yet,
> Lest we forget -- lest we forget!
>
> For heathen hear that puts her trust
> In reeking tube and iron shard,
> All valiant dust that builds on dust,
> And guarding calls not thee to guard
> For frantic boast and foolish word --
> Thy mercy on thy people, Lord.[25]

Kipling's hymn comes from a long time of hymns that express
similar sentiments wholly or in part. Enjoying the status of
one of the oldest such hymns is "Jerusalem my happy home"
believed to have been written about 1616, and signed in
manuscript form, "F.B.P." and, therefore, attributed to Francis

Baker, Priest.[26] The hymn is in use today in a much altered
form. The original version, consisting of six stanzas,
includes the following:

> Thy gardens and thy gallant walkes
>   Continually are greene;
> There growe such sweete and pleasant flowers
>   As noe where else are seene.
>
> There's nectar and ambrosia made
>   There's muske and civette sweete,
> There manie a fair and daintie drugge
>   Are trodden under feete.
>
> There cinnamon, there sugar grows,
>   There nard and balm abound:
> What tongue can tell or heart conceive
>   The joys that there are found.[27]

Clearly, a reference to the newly established tropical colonies
of the British Empire, these stanzas mention the rich spices
that had changed the taste and texture of English cuisine. In
addition to this internal historical reference, these stanzas
also reflect a popular seventeenth-century secular concern: the
belief that plants were the source of valuable drugs. A
seventeenth-century English congregation, therefore, could well
understand such a secular reference. In its current form,
"Jerusalem my happy home" retains only its initial stanza.
The other four stanzas reflect rearrangement, paraphrase an
summary of the original hymn. The tone of excitement and
discovery, present in the original version, seems subdued in
this latter form:

> Jerusalem, my happy home,
>   Name ever dear to me,
> When shall my labours have an end?

Thy joys when shall I see?

When shall these eyes thy heaven-built walls
    And pearly gates behold?
Thy bulwarks with salvation strong,
    And streets of shining gold?

Apostles, Martyrs, Prophets, there
    Around my Savior stand;
And all I love in Christ below
    Will join the glorious band.

Jerusalem, my happy home,
    When shall I come to thee?
When shall my labours have an end?
    Thy joys when shall I see?

O Christ, do Thou my soul prepare
    For that bright home of love;
That I may see thee and adore,
    With all thy saints above.[28]

Upholding the postulation that the nationalistic hymn had

its roots in seventeenth-century hymnody is George Herbert's

popular hymn the "Antiphon," or "Let all the world in every

corner sing." Intact in its original form, the "Antiphon" is

sung today:

Let all the world in every corner sing,
        My God and King!
    The heavens are not too high,
    His praise may thither fly;
    The earth is not too low,
    His praises there may grow.
Let all the world in every corner sing
My God and King

Let all the world in every corner sing,
        My God and King
    The church with psalms must shout,
    No door can keep them out;
    But above all, the heart
    Must bear the longest part.
Let all the world in every corner sing,
    My God and King![29]

This hymn is called the "Antiphon" because of its antiphonal
arrangement into chorus and verse. The hymn also makes much of
the fact that God is accessible to people in every corner of
the world. Also, in Stanza II, the hymn writer injects a
popular concern, "the church with psalms must shout/No doors
can keep them out," a blunt statement of Herbert's own
conviction and a reference to the current controversy
concerning the singing of hymns during church worship.

As was stated above, these nationalistic seventeenth-
century hymns blazed the trail for later hymn writers who
followed in suit. Notable among hymn writers of this category
is Joseph Addison (1672-1719), best known as an essayist.
Addison amplified the canon of seventeenth-century English
hymns that reflect imperial concerns. Of Addison, Millar
Patrick says:

> Joseph Addison stands beyond the group of
> preparers of the way . . . yet in his staid
> and formal fashion he had part in the same
> movement. It may seem strange that the wit
> and essayist, the gentle and polished
> satirist of contemporary manners, the man of
> the world and Secretary of State should stand
> with hymn writers at all. Yet he is by no
> means out of place in such company . . . he
> was a devout Christian, and John Wesley bears
> witness that by his exposure of the folly,
> and worse, of many of the social customs of
> his time, he rendered signal service to the
> kingdom of God. Anything like enthusiasm in
> religion was regarded with horror then, and
> Addison's hymns "The spacious firmament on
> high" . . . and "When all thy mercies O, my
> God" . . . have the quality of their age in
> being restrained, cool, never quite warming
> to life.[30]

In addition to the marked seventeenth-century style and
tone observed by Patrick, Addison's hymns contain specific
references to the secular concerns of the late seventeenth
century. Writing with perhaps only second-hand knowledge,
Addison, in the "Traveller's Hymn," writes of the colonies:

> Thy mercy sweetened every soil,
> Made every region please,
> The hoary Alpine hills it warmed,
> And smoothed the Tyrrhene seas.

and also,

> How are thy servants blessed, O, Lord!
> How sure is their defense!
> Eternal wisdom is their guide,
> Their help, Omnipotence.
>
> In foreign realms and lands remote
> Supported by they care
> Through burning climes they pass unhurt
> And breathe in tainted air.[31]

Although this hymn ostensibly shows God's omnipotence, it also
shows the prevailing, somewhat condescending, attitude towards
foreign lands, an attitude that prevailed through the
eighteenth century into the nineteenth. These brief stanzas by
Alexander Pope (1688-1744) also attest a similar notion:

> Father of all, in every age
> In every clime adored;
> By saint, by savage and by sage
> Jehovah, Jove our Lord.

Again, Pope writes of foreigners as barbarians, thereby showing
some degree of xenophobia which may have been common in England
in the seventeenth century and is seen also in literary works
such as Shakespeare's Othello Pope's lyric reads:

> See barbarous nations at thy gates attend,
> Walk in thy light and in thy temple bend;
> See thy bright altars thronged with prostrate kings
> While every land its joyful tribute brings.[32]

A century later, George Washington Doane wrote in a similar

vein:

> Fling out the banner, heathen lands
> Shall see from far the glorious sight
> And nations crowding to be born
> Baptize their spirits in its light.[33]

Beginning in the seventeenth century, a line of hymns referring

to the contemporary imperial concerns gave rise to a category

of hymns that now represents a preferred collection including

such favorites as Reginald Heber's hymn "From Greenland's icy

mountains." The opening stanzas read as follows:

> From Greenland's icy mountains,
> From India's coral strand,
> Where Afric's sunny fountains
> Roll down their golden sand,
> From many an ancient river,
> From many a palmy plain,
> They call us to deliver
> Their land from errors chain.
>
> Can we, whose souls are lighted
> With wisdom from on high,
> Can we to men benighted
> The lamp of life deny
> Salvation, O salvation!
> The joyful sound proclaim,
> Till each remotest nation
> Has learnt Messiah's name.[34]

This missionary hymn, composed upon assumptions similar to

those of the seventeenth-century imperialists, puts forth the

pervading belief that the Englishman is enlightened with divine

wisdom and that the colonized peoples "benighted" and backward.

Although most seventeenth-century hymn writers were quick
to observe and utilize contemporary secular concerns related to
colonialism, very little notice was given to institutional
slavery that was attendant upon that colonialism. For this
reason, Nahum Tate (1652-1715) stands out among the other hymn
writers, for he shows humane concern for slaves. Nahum Tate, a
translater of Psalms, and writer of hymns, best known for his
contribution to the "New Version" of the Psalter (1696), draws
attention to the secular concern of slavery in his hymn
"Captivity":

> When we our wearied limbs to rest,
> Sat down by proud Euphrates' stream,
> Se slept, with doleful thoughts oppressed,
> And Zion was our mournful theme.
>
> How shall we tune our voice to sing,
> Or touch our harps with skillful hands?
> Shall hymns of joy to God our King
> Be sung by slaves in foreign lands.[35]

Beginning with a carefully chosen title, "Captivity," Tate
gradually builds up a subtle argument that is anti-slavery. He
focuses his attention on the constrictions of captivity by
showing in Stanza I that the Children of Israel were weary,
oppressed and unhappy while they were in captivity. The hymn
writer makes reference to the opening lines of Psalm CXXXVII:
"By the rivers of Babylon, there we sat down, yea, we wept,
when we remembered Zion," to demonstrate the wrongs of
slavery. The strong impact of such a quotation on churchgoing
Englishmen must not be overlooked, for these were the times in

which every Biblical remark was held in the highest esteem.
Continuing his case, the hymn writer then asks a two-part
rhetorical question of the singers -- that is to say, how can
they, knowing the exigencies of slavery, offer songs and music
to God and remain oblivious to the sufferings of slave?
Furthermore, how can slaves in foreign lands sing "hymns" of
joy when slavery offers no joyous opportunities?

Of vital importance to this study is a reference such as
Tate's, for not only does it show a current interest in the
seventeenth-century secular concern of slavery, and the
imperialist notion of expansion in the name of missionary
services in the colonies newly won, but also it carries
internal evidence that the singing of hymns had probably been
promulgated even then to the colonies. The former must have
been of general interest in the seventeenth century because
slavery directly contributed to the well-being of the new and
growing empire and to the wealth of several English families.
Although this situation might have been well-known, few, if
any other hymn writers viewed slavery from what could be here
described as a Christian viewpoint. Nahum Tate's direct attack
upon institutionalized slavery is a unique one. Even among
later hymn writers the reference to slavery are of a different
nature. For example, John Newton (1725-1807),[36] clearly not a
seventeenth century man, was a prolific hymn writer who was
himself a slave trader.[37] Even among the hymns of a man who

had first-hand experience with slavery, no such direct
reference is observed. In fact, the scattered and oblique
references to slavery that one uncovers in Newton's hymns are
usually expressions of concerns for the well-being of his soul
as the stanzas below demonstrate:

> Come my soul thy suit prepare,
> Jesus loves to answer prayer;
> He himself has bid thee pray,
> Therefore will not say thee nay
>
> Thou art coming to a King
> Large petitions with thee bring;
> For his grace and power are such
> None can ever ask too much
>
> With my burden I begin:
> Lord remove this load of sin;
> Let thy blood for sinners split,
> Set my conscience free from guilt.[38]

In Stanza III, the hymn writer pleads for the absolution of his
guilt-burdened conscience. While this type of plea is common
place in prayers and the like, it appears that guilt is a
dominant concern with the reformed slave trader. The following
hymn by Newton is of similar nature:

> In evil long I took delight
>   Unawed by shame or fear,
> Till a new object struck my sight
>   And stopped my wild career.
>
> I saw one hanging on a tree,
>   In agonies and blood;
> He fixed his languid eyes on me,
>   As near his cross I stood.
> Oh, never, till my latest breath
>   Shall I forget that look!
> It seemed to charge me with his death.
>   Though not a word he spoke.
>
> . . . .

182

> Thus, while his death my sin displays
>   In all its blackest hue,
> Such is the mystery of grace,
>   It seals my pardon too.[39]

By examining the development of this hymn, one may arrive
at the conclusion that Newton lived to realize the atrocities
of his "wild career." In Stanza I, he admits that he suffered
no remorse or fear until he experienced salvation. The second
and third stanzas refer to the crucified Christ, but the image
could easily be that of a mistreated slave. In any case,
however, the hymn keeps its meaning. These references to the
images of bondage and slavery are common ones in Christianity
for often sin and life without salvation are referred to as
bondage and salvation treated as freedom. Newton applies the
concept of slavery to the entire world. This concept is shown
in his hymn "Savior, Visit Thy plantation." The opening stanza
reads:

> Savior visit thy plantation;
>   Grant us, Lord, a gracious rain;
> All will come to desolation
>   Unless Thou return again.[40]

The fact that John Newton wrote in this vein almost a century
later than Nahum Tate, enhances Tate's more sensitive awareness
of the seventeenth-century humanistic problem of slavery.
Newton, emerging from the age of reason, uses his personal
experience as the source of his metaphor. Yet, as distasteful
as it is today to view God's kingdom as a plantation, and as
incongruous as it seems to imagine God a slave master, these

concepts were tolerable to that hymn writer because he probably lacked the empathy displayed by the seventeenth-century hymn writer, Nahum Tate, who lived in a society that offered him less than total religious freedom.

With full knowledge of the pleasures of the salubrious climate of the tropical colonies, some seventeenth-century hymn writers revealed their interest in the secular matters of their day. Andrew Marvell (1621-1678), a metaphysical poet, famous for his lyrical verse, wrote "Song to the Emigrants of Bermuda." Although this song is not in common use, it is listed among sacred songs of the seventeenth century, and it is rich in its references to secular concerns. The "song" reads:

> Where the remote Bermudas ride
> In the ocean's bosom unespied
> From a small boat that row'd along
> The listening winds receive this song:
> What should we do but sing His praise
> That led us through the watery maze.
>
> Where he the huge sea monster wracks
> That lifts the deep upon their backs
> Unto an isle so long unknown
> And yet far kinder than our own?
>
> He lands us on a grassy stage
> Safe from the storms and prelate's rage
> He gave us this eternal Spring
> Which here enamels everything.
>
> He cast (of which we rather boast)
> The Gospels pearl upon our coast;
> And in these rocks for us did frame
> A temple where we sound His name.
>
> O let our voice His praise exhalt
> Till it arrive at Heaven's vault,
> Which thence (perhaps) rebounding may
> Echo beyond the Mexique bay.[41]

In overt terms, this sacred song reveals much that was typical of seventeenth-century English life. First, reference is made to the small row-boat, dependent upon kind winds, a reference to the use of row-boats for transport from ship to shore over waters often hazardous. Also, the sea is metaphorically termed the "watery maze" for sailing as a precise science was still in developmental stages. The song writer, therefore, owes the safe sighting of the Bermudas to God and his powerful guidance and not to the mariner's compass and such other nautical apparatuses as maps and charts that were at his disposal.

In Stanza II, one sees the seventeenth-century mythical explanation of the tides. The misconception or the belief that huge sea monsters lived in the deeps and that their activities below gave rise to the movement of the surface waters is openly stated. It must be remembered that it was Sir Isaac Newton (1642-1727) who, in the second and third book of the Pricipia (1687), explained the tidal peculiarities as they relate to gravity. The above reference to sea monsters fits the pattern of pagan beliefs earlier mentioned and demonstrates to a large extent yet another vital secular concern of the age.

Enlightening though these references to monsters and witches may be, it is the geographical and political-religious references which seem to give a real link between the English hymn and other seventeenth-century literature reflecting

popular concerns. For instance, this sacred song identifies
the Bermudas as the location, and the hymn writer admits that
it is "a land far kinder" than their own England. It is a land
where the "eternal spring" "enamels everything." Obviously,
the beauty and the mild weather of the tropical colonies were
of contemporary interest in England. Not to be overlooked is
Shakespeare's reference to the tropical storms and the Bermudas
in his play The Tempest. In this play, Ariel, Prospero's
spirit-servant, reports to him on the assignment that Prospero
had delegated to him. Ariel reports:

> Jove's lightnings, the precursors
> O' the dreadful thunderclaps, more momentary
> And sight-outrunning were not; the fire and cracks
> Of sulphurous roaring the most mighty Neptune
> Seem to beseige, and make his bold waves tremble,
> Yea, his dread strident shake.
>
> . . . .
>
> Safely in the harbour
> Is the King's ship; in the deep nook, where once
> Thou call'st me up at midnight to fetch dew
> From the still-vex'd Bermoothes, there she's hid.[42]
> (I. i. 201-230.)

The Cambridge History of English Literature claims that
Shakespeare's main source for the setting of The Tempest came
from Sir George Somer's book, Bermuda (1609).[43] Most
important, though, is the realization that the seventeenth-
century hymn remained meaningful in its day. Hardly an aspect
of English secular life goes unmentioned in the hymns of that
century.

Bringing the hymn to an equally relevant climax, Marvell

acknowledges God's goodness in landing the seekers of religious freedom in a land where they are safe from "the storms and the prelate's rage"; that is to say, they are rid of church strife and its attendant polemics. They are now free to spread God's word, "the pearl" in this remote colony, and thereby erect a memorial of praise. Their joyful songs will echo beyond the "Mexique bay," a final reference to the geographical explorations which were then at their peak. The Mexican Bay and the Caribbean area had been of major importance to the English seadogs, the pirates, the imperialist explores such as Sir Francis Drake, Sir Walter Raleigh, and Richard Hawkins who indulged in treasure-hunting off the Spanish Main. Several of these men produced books[44] about the new world that were popular in England; hence the interest in Eldorado was real to seventeenth-century English people and the influence of these works was constantly manifested in the literature.

Soon this new materialistic interest manifested itself in the seventeenth-century English hymn. Transferring materialism and imperialism into images, the hymn writer changed even the concept of heaven. Instead of a pastoral heaven, blessed with milk and honey, streams and peaceful pastures, heaven become a guilded city (The Eldorado Myth). The Arcadian Elizabethan heaven gave way to a rich and ornamented place. Stanzas from "Jerusalem, my happy home" speak for themselves:

> Thy walls are made of precious stones
> Thy bulwarks diamondes square

Thy gates of right orient pearle
Exceeding rich and rare.

Thy turrettes and thy pinnacles
With carbuncles do shine;
Thy verrie streets are paved with gould
Surpassing clear and fine.

Thy houses are of yvorie,
Thy windows crystal cleare
Thy tyles are made of beaten gould
O God, that I were there.[45]

Although this latest direction of the hymn suggests God's
sanction of imperialistic trends as a mere expansion of his
kingdom on earth, this seventeenth-century hymn also shows the
hymn writer's ability to expand its base, thus revealing
variety, change and growth in the matter of the English hymn.
New and old myths found peaceful union and hymn writers ended
the century with a sense of achievement. No longer were hymns
restricted to inspiration from the Psalms on spiritual
experiences, but rather other aspects of secular life were
looked at as sources of inspiration.

In viewing the spectrum of the seventeenth-century hymn,
one sees clear traces of the scientific philosophical,
sociological, and geographical concerns of the age. Not
readily apparent to some hymn singers today, several of these
ideas lie buried or shrouded in a particular hymn, requiring
special knowledge and understanding of seventeenth-century
English life before they yield their rich, full meanings.

188

NOTES FOR CHAPTER V

[1]According to Sir Oliver Lodge, (Pioneers of Science, p. 58) Kepler, though a German, dedicated, in 1620, his work On Celestial Harmonies, explaining the relationship between time and distance to King James of England. Also, in that same year, Kepler's mother was tortured for witchcraft, a practice common in Europe and America in those days.

[2]James Broderick, S. J. Galileo and the Roman Inquisition (London: Catholic Truth Society, 1963), p. 34.

[3]Allan-Olney, Mary, compiler, The Private Life of Galileo, Compiled from his Correspondence and that of his Eldest Daughter (London: McMillan and Co., 1870), pp. 74-75.

[4]Sir Oliver Lodge, Pioneers of Science and the Development of their Scientific Theories (New York: Dover Publications, 1960).

[5]The English Hymnal, revised edition (London: Oxford University Press, 1933), No. 577.

[6]The Harvard University Hymn Book (Cambridge: Harvard University Press, 1926), No. 294.

[7]McDonald, England's Antiphon (London: Macmillan and Co., 1874), p. 158.

[8]McDonald, England's Antiphon, p. 157.

[9]F. T. Palgrave, Treasury of Sacred Song, p. 22

[10]Edgar Newgrass, Melody in Your Heart: A Concise History of Hymnology (Bushey Heath, Hertfordshire: A. E. Callam, 1964), p. 11.

[11]Alexander C. Judson, Seventeenth Century Lyrics (Chicago: University of Chicago Press, 1927), p. vi.

[12]The Hymnal of the Protestant Episcopal Church in the United States of America (New York: Church Pension Fund, 1940), No. 476.

[13]Neo-platonism was an attempt to combine philosophy with religion, an attempt to reconstruct old beliefs in the light of new knowledge. Henry More also a hymn writer and Lord Herbert of Cherbury, brother of George Herbert were the leading

advocates of neo-platonism. Below is an excerpt from Herbert's work De Veritate, translated from Latin by Basil Willey, explaining the attempt to seek a common denominator for all religions, and, thus, provide a settlement to religious disputes of the seventeenth century: "Thus universal consent will be the sovereign test of truth, and there is nothing of so great importance as to seek out the common notions and to put them each in their place as indubitable truths. This is more necessary now than ever, for since it is not only by arguments that we are confused . . . poor mortals, astonished by these fulminations, have no refuge unless we establish certain unshakable foundations of truth supported by universal consent, to which they can have recourse in the doubts of Theology or of Philosophy," from Basil Willey's "Rational Theology Lord Herbert," The Seventeenth Century Background: Studies in the Thought of an Age in Relation to Poetry and Religion (London: Chatto and Windus, 1942), p. 123.

[14]Bailey, Gospel in Song, p. 27

[15]George Herbert, "Cambridge Poems," The English Works of George Herbert, Vol. II, ed. G. H. Palmer (Boston: Houghton Mifflin and Co., 1905), pp. 99-101.

[16]Homer Rodheaver, Hymnal Handbook for Standard Hymns and Gospel Songs (Chicago and Philadelphia: The Rodheaver Co., 1975), p. 80.

[17]Harvey B. Marks, The Rise and Growth of English Hymnody (New York: Flemming H. Revell Co., 1937), p. 87.

[18]Simonds, History of English Literature, p. 206.

[19]The English Hymnal, No. 410.

[20]Robert Herrick, The Poetical Works of Robert Herrick ed. L. C. Martin (Oxford: The Clarendon Press, 1956), pp. 247-248.

[21]Thomas Campion was one of the first composers to publish his music in book form. In 1601, he published his Book of Airs. It is possible that hymns were sung to some of his tunes, since a few early hymns were set to traditional English melodies.

[22]Thomas Campion, A Book of Airs (London: 1601), Air XVIII.

[23]Palgrave, Treasury of Sacred Song, pp. 20-21.

190

24Herbert A. Jefferson, <u>Hymns in Christian Worship</u> (London: Rockliff, 1950), p. 21.

25<u>The Hymnal of the Protestant Episcopal Church</u>, No. 147, <u>The Works of Rudyard Kipling</u> (New York: Black's REaders Service Co., n.d.), p. 15.

26Horder, <u>The Hymn Lover</u>, p. 81.

28<u>Hymns Ancient and Modern</u>, No. 236.

29George Herbert, <u>Bemerton Poems</u>, p. 63 and <u>The Clarendon Hymn Book</u>, No. 212. It is possible that this hymn influenced Charles Wesley's writing of a similar hymn "Let Saints on Earth in concert sing/With those whose work is done/For all the servants of our King/In earth and heaven are on." This hymn carries the egalitarian attitude expressed in some of Herbert's hymns and Wesley was a well-known admirer of George Herbert.

30Patrick, <u>The Story of the Church's Song</u>, (Richmond: John Knox Press, 1962), p. 120.

31Hatfield, <u>The Church Hymn Book</u>, p. 83.

32Charles Richards, <u>Songs of Christian Praise</u> (New York: Taintor Brothers, Merrill and Co., 1880), p. 291.

33<u>The Hymnal of the Protestant Episcopal Church</u>, No. 259.

34<u>The Episcopal Hymnal</u>, No. 254.

35<u>The Church Hymn Book</u>, p. 426.

36John Newton, while curate at Olney in Buckinghamshire published 280 hymns in conjunction with 68 hymns of William Cowper. <u>The Olney Hymns</u> was printed in 1779.

37F. A. Jones, <u>Famous Hymns</u>, pp. 316-317.

38Evangelical <u>Lutheran Hymn Book</u>, No. 56.

39<u>The Baptist Hymnal</u>, No. 294.

40<u>The Baptist Hymnal</u>, No. 565.

41F. T. Palgrave, <u>Treasury of Sacred Song</u>, p. 77.

42William G. Clarke and William Wright, eds., <u>The Plays and Sonnets of William Shakespeare, II</u> (London: Encyclopedia Britannica, Inc., 1952), p. 527.

43"Literature of the Sea," <u>Cambridge History of English Literature, IV</u> (Cambridge: Cambridge University Press, 1909), p. 78.

44Among the best known of these books are:
Sir Walter Raleigh, <u>The Discovery of Guiana</u> (1596).
Richard Hakluyt, <u>The Principall Navigations</u> (1589).
Sir George Somers, <u>Bermuda</u> (1609).
Richard Hawkins, <u>Observations</u> (1622).

45Horder, <u>The Hymn Lover</u>, p. 81.

CONCLUSION

To study the seventeenth-century English hymn is to study, partially, seventeenth-century thought. This major purpose of this work was to investigate the English hymn as a mode for sacred and secular concerns and it has been revealed that the hymn has been an effective vehicle for those political, social, scientific and religious concerns. Although the seventeenth-century hymn writers were novices in one respect, their hymns deal with a wide range of subjects, many of which have no relevance to present-day hymn singers, but serve, nonetheless, to show the roots of English hymnody. With equal conviction, the seventeenth-century English hymn bears evidence of history. Close study of the hymn reveals that significant reference is made to incidents of the age, veiled and indirect though some references might be.

With religious freedom threatened by sovereign decrees in seventeenth-century England, the hymn writer became a poet expressing his private doubts and beliefs. In time, what was the private doubt of one writer became the common fears of large groups of citizens. Thus, the hymn writer, it is revealed, sometimes became a spokesman for a particular political or religious sect. This study has also revealed hymns that opposed religious doctrines of the Church of England as well as hymns that supported those doctrines. The same situation existed for Protestant and Roman Catholic doctrines.

194

Indeed, one of the important findings of this research is the existence of the type of hymn that could be termed "counterdoctrinal," a term meaning a type of hymn that does not strongly support a particular doctrine, but which, by logical reasoning, attempts to refute one or more doctrines.

In the realm of the sacred concerns of the seventeenth-century English hymn, this research has shown that the hymn is a mode through which the individual religious right of the Christian could be asserted. The hymn, therefore, touches, at times, upon the spiritual autobiography of the writer, as is the case with John Bunyan, Thomas Ken, and Cardinal Newman. Beyond this application, these hymns serve as a medium for the religious or spiritual education of the masses, that is to say, they openly espoused dogmatic and didactic tenets, and, in rare instances, suggested the appropriate reward or punishment for the supporter or the objector.

Not only did the seventeenth-century hymn promulgate Calvinistic, Anglican, and Catholic tenets, but it simplified these doctrines and offered them in a form which rendered them easily comprehensible and memorable. As is the case with secular concerns, the seventeenth-century hymn shows the conflict between older religious beliefs such as Apostolic Succession and the then contemporary injunctions such as the Divine Right of Kings, or the older concept of a God of wrath opposed to the newer concept of a God of love. As seventeenth-century religious thought grew, changed, and solidified, so too did the English hymn.

Probably the most pervasive politico-religious theme in the seventeenth-century hymn is that of the fragmentation of the church. In this respect, a close relationship is seen between the seventeenth-century hymn and the general body of English literature, for the schism in the Church remained the theme of many poems and prose works of the seventeenth and eighteenth centuries.

Because no clear lines of demarcation exist between the politics and religion of the seventeenth-century Englishman, it becomes possible to interpret several hymns within the framework of political and religious upheavals. Indeed, this study reveals that the seventeenth-century hymn writers who composed the hymns termed here as "political" seem to have provided logical forerunners for the later body of militaristic and nationalistic hymns. Additionally, these hymns provided a platform from which political opponents, even the King, could be attacked, or from which one could defend his own political stance, always with the over-riding conviction that God was on the hymn writer's side, whatever that side might be.

Ironically, this research shows evidence that even the English hymns of praise and contentment of the seventeenth century may have their base in political concerns. Praising God for granting victory over enemies was a popular theme then.

Also, it was shown that one's contentment was relative to one's political status. Contentment depended on whether Royalists, the king's forces, or Protestants, the opposing forces, were in command. Thus, the Puritan Interlude (1642-1660), brought forth a spate of hymns from PUritan writers who expressed their contentment in hymns such as Milton's still-famous "Let us with a gladsome mind."

Observing secular concerns in the seventeenth-century English hymn is a convoluted process, for often the expression of such a concern is an indirect one. In times of war, for instance, some hymn writers wrote of peace and love in such impressive hymns as Vaughan's "My Soul there is a Country," and in times of relative peace, some hymn writers wrote of war. This situation leaves the scholar to conclude that the hymn was probably used as an incentive to quicken men's hearts to goodness and to appeal to their reason, so that by emphasizing the discomforts of war during times of peace, hymn singers would refrain from warfare. By highlighting the pleasures of peace during a war, embattled factions would subdue their ire because the war, though purely ideological and verbal at times, was always religious and political.

Marking the opening of the modern scientific era, the seventeenth century stands between the old superstitions of the Middle Ages and the enlightenment of the Scientific Age. Graphically recorded in the seventeenth century English hymn is

this transition. The numerous scientific discoveries--the
heliocentric theory, the new science itself, physics,
astronomy, mathematics, chemistry, geography, newly discovered
lands, new colonies, new substances, new philosophical theories
such as neo-platonism-served as grist to the hymn writer's mill
to emerge as monuments of praise to God for his bounty. On the
other hand, acknowledging some of the lingering doubts,
superstitions or "Vulgar errors" to quote Sir Thomas Browne,
supplied the theme of another type of seventeenth-century hymn.
Free mention is made in these hymns of witchcraft, goblins,
evil spirits, devils, magic, witches, old astrological beliefs,
and alchemy. These beliefs, at times, persisted even in hymns
where newer beliefs appear, thus reflecting the transitional
nature of the times as well as the overwhelming concern with
secular matters.

Finally, to answer some of the specific questions that this
study asked, one has to agree that Watts could have compiled a
hymnbook from existing materials. Now it can be postulated
that if the title "Father of the English Hymn" goes to Isaac
Watts, then to the earlier seventeenth-century hymn writers
must be designated the honor of the title, grand-father of the
English hymn. Indeed, these original hymn writers, many of
whom are little known today, came mainly from three areas of
English life: the church, the court, and the school or
university, and in their separate ways each fought for the

198

legitimacy of the hymn. Because of the diversity in the
sources of the hymns, and probably because much emphasis was
placed on the mode for its utilitarian values, no clearly-
defined school of hymn writers is identifiable. It is safe to
conclude, nevertheless, that the seventeenth-century hymn
writers emerged from the same sources which provided other
English literary artists. Consequently, there is strong
similarity in the themes of the hymns and the general body of
seventeenth-century literature. Common seventeenth-century
forms were poems, plays, tracts, travelogues, devotions and
essays. The seventeenth-century hymn is not limited to any
single literary matter. Indeed it has cut across these lines
to enter the domain of literature, taking as its subject matter
both sacred and secular concerns, all of which have their
counterparts in the common literary forms of the century.

After a study of the English hymns, one is compelled to
agree with the view on hymns set forth by Henry Augustine
Smith:

> Those who sing from hymn books today are
> fast becoming students of lyric religion,
> searchers after the hidden treasures, its
> factual history, its romance and biography,
> its geographic and international
> implications, its interest to the foreign
> traveler, its brilliant metaphors and
> pictures and drama, its processions,
> coronations and reformation, its call to
> battle and peace after victory , its shrines
> of worship, in short the spiritual experience
> of the human race through all ages.[1]

---

[1] Henry Augustine Smith, Lyric Religion, p. v.

The seventeenth century English Hymn remains as one of the rich repositories of man's sacred and secular concerns.

APPENDIX A

In a lengthy treatise on "Christian Doctrine", Milton
questioned the foundation of the Catholic and Anglican Churches
as follows:

> How could a foundation have any
> successors? As for that famous text, Matt.
> xvi, 18, 19, which the Poper perverts in
> order to make it the letters patent of his
> papacy, it confers nothing on Peter which he
> does not share with anyone else who professes
> the same faith . . . So Christ's answer is
> not on you, Peter, but on this rock, or in
> other words, on this faith which you have in
> common with other believers.[1]

The text states:

> And I say unto thee, that thou are Peter, and
> upon this rock I will build my church; and
> the gates of hell shall not prevail against
> it.
>
> And I will give unto thee the keys of the
> kingdom of heaven: and whatsoever thou shalt
> bind on earth shall be bound in heaven: and
> whatsoever thou shalt loose on earth shall be
> loosed in heaven.

_____

[1]The Complete Prose Works of John Milton, Vol. VI (New
Haven: Yale University Press, 1973), p. 567.

APPENDIX B

The Act of Uniformity, 1662:

    The Act of Uniformity passed in 1662 by
the English Parliament required all clergy
man to declare their approval "of the
doctrine and worship of the Church of
England," and to submit "to the government
thereof as by law established . . . . Take
thou authority to preach the word of God and
administer the Sacraments and to perform all
ministerial offices in this Church of
England." The obstacle to agreement as
indispensable to ministry and in consenting
to all "nascent ceremonies" of the Prayer
Book. Two thousand clergymen resigned and
were excluded from holding benefice. From
then on all who refused to assent were called
dissenters.[2]

---

[2]Ruth Rose and Stephen C. Neil, _A History of the Ecumenical Movement, 1517-1948_ (London: S.P.C.K., 1967), p. 148.

APPENDIX C

CHRONOLOGICAL TABLE OF ENGLISH HYMN-WRITERS

A.D. 1400-1600

Miles Coverdale, Ep., 1488-1569
George Gascoigne, Ep., 1536 (?)-1577
Thomas Sternhold, Ep., d. 1549
Rev. John Hopkins, Ep., fl. 1551
Rev. William Kethe, P., 1510-1580
John Marckant, Ep., fl. 1562
John Mardley, Ep., fl. 1562
Sir Walter Raleigh, Ep., 1552-1618
Robert Southwell, R.C., 1560-1595
Sir Henry Wotton, Ep., 1568-1639
Sir John Davies, Ep., 1570-1626
John Donne, D.D., Ep., 1573-1637
Bishop Joseph Hall, D.D., Ep., 1574-1656
George Sandys, Ep., 1577-1643
Francis Rous, P., 1579-1658 (s.)
David Dickson, P., 1583-1663 (s)
Sir John Beaumont, Ep., 1856-1616
Sir William Drummond, Ep., 1585-1649 (s)
Rev. Giles Fletcher, Ep., 1588-1623
George Wither, P., 1588-1687
Robert Herrick, Ep., 1591-1674
Francis Quarles, P., 1592-1644
Rev. George Herbert, Ep., 1593-1632
Bp. John Cosin, Ep., 1594-1672

A.D. 1600-1700

Rev. Henry Jessey, B., 1601-1663
Sir Thomas Browne, Ep., 1605-1682
Edmund Waller, Ep., 1605-1687
John Milton, P., 1608-1674
Bp. Jeremy Taylor, Ep., 1613-1667
Henry More, D.D., Ep., 1614-1687
Rev. Richard Baxter, Ind., 1615-1691
Richard Crashaw, R.C., 1616(?)-1650(?)
"F.B.P." (Francis Baker, Priest ?) R.C., fl. 1616
Andrew Marvell, Ep., 1620-1678
Henry Vaughan, M.D., Ep., 1621-1695 (w.)
Rev. John Mason, Ep., d. 1694
John Quarles, P., 1624-1665
John Austin, R.C., 1613-1669
Rev. John Bunyan, B., 1628-1688
Rev. Samuel Crossman, Ep., 1624-1683

John Dryden, R.C., 1631-1700
Wentworth Dillon, Earl Roscommon, Ep. (I.) 1633-1684.
Bp. Thomas Ken, Ep., 1637-1711
John Lagniel, 16 -1728
Nahum Tate, Ep., 1652-1715 (I.)
Rev. Nicholas Brady, D.D., Ep., 1659-1726 (I.)
Rev. Samuel Wesley, Sen., Ep., 1662-1735
Rev. Joseph Stennett, B., 1663-1713
Rev. Thomas Shepherd, Cong., 1665-1739
Joseph Addison, Ep., 1672-1719
Mrs. Elizabeth (Singer) Rowe, 1674-1737
Rev. Isaac Watts, Ind., 1674-1748
Rev. John Killinghall, Cong., d. 1740
Bp. John Patrick, Ep., fl. 1679
Rev. Simon Browne, Ind., 1680 (?)-1732
Rev. James Craig, P., 1682-1744 (s.)
Alexander Pope, R.C., 1688-1744
Robert Cruttenden, Ind., 1690-1763
Samuel Wesley, Jr., Ep., 1690-1739
Rev. William Robertson, Ep., d. 1743 (s.)
John Byrom, M.D., Ep., 1691-1763
Rev. Robert Seagrave, Ep., 1693-1759
Rev. John Taylor, P., 1694-1761
Rev. Robert Blair, Ep., 1699-1746 (s.)
Christopher Pitt, 1699-1748
Rev. William Barton, Ep. 1598 (?)-1678

Source: Samuel W. Duffield English Hymns, Their Authors & History Funk & Wagnals (London: 1886), pp. 625-626.

A SELECTED BIBLIOGRAPHY

Allan-Olney, Mary. The Private Life of Galileo Compiled from His Correspondence and that of His Eldest Daughter. London: McMillan and Co., 1870.

A Collection of Hymns for the Use of the Protestant Church of the United Brethren. Philadelphia: I Ashmead and Co., 1832.

Bailey, Edward Albert. The Gospel in Hymns: Background and Interpetations. New York: Charles Scribners and Sons, 1950

Baugh, Albert C. A History of the English Language, 2nd ed. Englewood Cliffs, New Jersey: Prentice Hall, 1957.

Baxter, Richard. The Causes, Evils and Cure of Church Divisions ed., Francis Asbury. New York: Lane and Scott, 1849.

_____. The Poetical Fragments with Sacred Hymns. London: printed for William Pickering, 1821.

Blair, Walter, Theodore Hornberger, Randall Steward and James E. Miller, Jr. The Literature of the United States, I. Chicago: Scott, Foresman and Co., 1953.

Benson, Louis F. The English Hymn: Its Development and Use in Worship. Richmond, Virginia: John Knox Press, 1962 (reprint).

_____. The Hymnody of the Christian Church, New York: George H. Doran Co., 1927.

_____. "The Hymns of John Bunyan," Papers of the Hymn Society of America, Paper no. 1. 1930.

Bratt, John H. The Rise and Development of Calvinism: Concise History. Grand Rapids, Michigan: William B. Erdman's Pub. Co., 1959.

Brawley, Benjamin. The History of the English Hymn. New York: the Abingdon Press, 1932.

Broderick, James. Galileo and the Roman Inquisition. London Catholic Truth Society, 1963.

Bunyan, John. Grace Abounding to the Chief of Sinners. ed., Roger Sharrock. Oxford: The Clarendon Press, 1962.

Bush, Douglas, _English Literature in the Earlier Seventeenth Century_. Oxford: Clarendon Press, 1964.

Campion, Thomas. _A Book of Airs_. London, 1601.

Carlyle, Thomas. ed. _The Letters and Speeches of Oliver Cromwell._ New York: AMS Press, 1945.

Chryssostom, John. _Manual of Christian Doctrine._ Philadelphia: John Joseph McVey, 1962.

Clarke, William G. and William Wright. eds. _The Plays and Sonnets of William Shakespeare._ London: Encyclopedia Britannica, Inc., 1952.

Davies, Horton. _The Worship of the English Puritans._ London: Dacre Press, 1948.

Dearmer, Percy. _The Story of the Prayer Book in the Old and New World and throughout the Anglican Church._ London: Oxford University Press, 1933.

Donne, John. _Complete Poetry and Selected Prose of John Donne_. New York: Random House, 1941.

Duffield, Samuel W. _English Hymns: Their Authors and History._ London: Funk and Wagnalls, 1886.

England, Martha W. and John Sparrow. _Hymns Unbidden_. New York: New York Public Library, 1966.

Farr, Edward, ed., _Select Poetry Chiefly Sacred of the Reign of Charles the First._ Cambridge: Cambridge University Press, 1847.

Gillman, Frederick John. _The Evolution of the English Hymn._ New York: Macmillan Co., 1927.

Green, John R. _A History of the English People._ III, 1603-1683. New York: Nottingham Society, n.d.

Green, John R. _A Short History of the English People._ London: Dutton, 1897.

Guoizot, M. Francois. _History of Oliver Cromwell and the English Commonwealth from the Execution of Charles I to the Death of Cromwell._ Andrew R. Scoble, Trans. Philadelphia: Blanchard and Lea, 1854.

Harvey, Sir Paul. The Oxford Companion to English Literature
4th ed. Oxford: University Press, 1967.

Harlow, Louis K. comp., The World's Best Hymns. Boston:
Little Brown and Co., 1894.

Hatfield, E. F. comp., The Church Hymn Book. New York:
Ivison, Blakeman, Taylor and Co., 1875.

Hatfield, E. F. The Poets of the Church. Boston:
Milford House, 1872.

Harvard University Hymn Book. Cambridge, Mass: Harvard
University Press, 1926.

Herbert, George. The English Works of George Herbert II
and III, ed. G. H. Palmer. Boston: Houghton Mifflin and
Co., 1905.

_____. Select Hymns Taken out of Mr. Herbert's Temple and
Turned into Common Metre to be Sung (originally published
by Thomas Parkhurs, 1697 London: Augustan Reprint Society,
Publication 98, 1962.

_____. The Works of George Herbert, ed. E. F. Hutchinson.
Oxford: Clarendon Press, 1941.

Herrick, Robert. The Poetical Works of Robert Herrick,
ed. L. C. Martin. Oxford: The Clarendon Press, 1956.

Horder, William Garrett. The Hymn Lover: An Account of
Rise and Growth of English Hymnody. London: J. Curwen and
Sons, c. 1889.

Hymnal Companion to the Prayer Book. Compiler, W. J. Boehm.
Philadelphia: Armstrong Keyser, 1907.

Jefferson, Herbert A. L. Hymns in Christian Worship. London:
Rockliff, 1950.

Johansen, John Henry. ed., The Olney Hymns. New York:
Hymn Society of America, reprint, 1956.

Jones, Francis Arthur. Famous Hymns and Their Authors London:
Hodder and Stroughton, 1905.

Judson, Alexander Corbin. ed. Seventeenth Century Lyrics.
Chicago: University of Chicago Press, 1927.

Julian, John. A Dictionary of Hymnology. London: John
    Murray, 1925.

Keach, Benjamin. War with the Devil: or the Young Man's
    Conflict with the Powers of Darkness. [In Dialogue]
    London: Printed for Benjamin Harris, 1695.

Kipling, Rudyard, The Works of Kipling. New York: Black's
    Readers' Service Co., n.d.

"Literature of the Sea," Cambridge History of English
    Literature, IV. Cambridge: Cambridge University Press,
    1909, pp. 78-79.

Lodge, Sir Oliver, Pioneers of Science and the Development of
    Their Scientific Theories New York: Dover Publication,
    1960.

Martz, Louis L. The Poetry of Meditation. New Haven:
    Yale University Press, 1954.

McDonald, George. England's Antiphon. London: Macmillan
    and Co. 1874.

Manning, Bernard L. The Hymns of Wesley and Watts: Five
    Informal Papers. London: The Epwroth Press, 1942.

Marks, Harvey B. The Rise and Growth of English Hymnody.
    New York: Flemming H. Revell Co., 1937.

Merryweather, Frank B. The Evolution of the Hymn. London:
    William Clowes and Sons, Ltd. 1966.

Milton, John. The Complete Poetry and Selected Prose of
    John Milton. ed., E. H. Visak. Glasgow: University
    Press, 1964.

_____. The Complete Prose Works of John Milton. VI.
    New Haven: Yale University Press, 1973.

_____. The Poetical Works of John Milton to which is
    Prefixed a Biography by his Nephew, Edward Phillips. New
    York: D. Appleton and Co., 1859.

_____. The Poetical Works of John Milton. ed. David Masson.
    London: Macmillan and Co., 1874.

Moravian Church. A Collection of Hymns of the Children of God
    in All Ages from the Beginning Till Now. London: 1754.

Moffatt, James and Millar Patrick. The Handbook to Church Hymnary. London: Oxford University Press, 1927.

Monk, William H. compiler, Hymns Ancient and Modern, London: William Clowes and Sons, Ltd., 1815.

Montgomery, James. The Christian Palmist or Hymns, Glasgow: William Collins c. 1825.

Neale, John Mason. Collected Hymnsa. London: Hodder and Stroughton, 1914.

Newgrass, Edgar. Melody in Your Heart: A Concise History of Hymnology. Hertfordshire: A. E. Callam, 1964.

Newman, John Henry. Apologia Pro Vita Sua: The Two Versions of 1964 and 1865. London: Oxford University Press, 1913.

Newton, John. Olney Hymns in Three Books. London: Thomas Tegg, 1779.

Ninde, Edward. Nineteen Centuries of Christian Song. New York: Fleming H. Revell Co. 1938.

Northcott, Cecil. Hymns in Christian Worship: The Use of Hymns in the Life of the Church. Richmond: John Knox Press, 1964.

Nutter, Charles S. and Wilbur F. Tillett, The Hymns and Hymn Writers of the Church. New York: Eaton and Mains, 1911.

Palgrave, Francis. The Treasury of Sacred Song Selected from the English Lyrical Poetry of Four Centuries. Oxford: Clarendon Press, 1890.

Parry, Graham. Seventeenth Century Poetry: The Social Context. London: Hutchinson and Co. Ltd. 1985.

Patrick, Millar. The Supplement to the Handbook to Church Hymnary. London: Oxford University Press, 1935.

_____. The Story of the Church's Song. Richmond: John Knox Press, 1962.

Poling, David. Songs of Faith: Signs of Hope. Waco, Texas: Word Books, 1976.

Pollard, Arthur. English Hymns. London: Longmans, Green and Co., 1960.

212

Pound, Louise. "Caedmon's Dream Song," Studies in English Philology (1929), p. 232.

Price, Carl F. "What is a Hymn?" Papers of the Hymn Society of America, no. 6, 1940.

Reeves, Jermiah Bascom. The Hymn as Literature. New York: The Century Co., 1924.

Reynolds, William J. A Survey of Christian Hymnody. New York: Holt Rinehart, and Winston, Inc., 1963.

Richards, Charles H. arranger. Songs of Christian Praise. New York: Tainter Bros. Merrill and Co., 1880.

Rodeheaver, Homer A. Hymnal Handbook for Standard Hymns and Gospel Songs. Chicago: The Rodeheaver Co., 1975.

Rouse, Ruth and Stephen C. Neil. A History of the Ecumenical Movement 1517-1948, London, SPCK, 1967.

Routley, Erik. Hymns and Human Life. Grand Rapids, Michigan: William Eerdmans Publishing Co., 1966.

Ryden, Ernest E. The Story of Christian Hymnody. Rock Island, Illinois: Augusta Press, 1959.

Saunders, Frederick. Evenings with the Sacred Poets. New York: T. Whittaker, 1899.

Saville, Rev. Bourchier. comp. Lyra Sacra: Being a Collection of Hymns Ancient and Modern. London: Longman, Green, London and Roberts, 1861.

Schelling, Felix E. The English Lyric. Reprint. Boston and New York: Riverside Press, Houghton and Mifflin, 1913.

Schmidt, Albert - Marie. John Calvin and the Calvinist Tradition. Trans., Ronald Wallace. New York: Harper and Brothers, 1960.

Simonds, William E. A History of English Literature. Boston: Houghton and Mifflin Co., 1902.

Smith, Henry Augustine. Lyric Religion: The Romance of the Immortal Hymns. London: The Century Co., 1931.

Stein, Arnold S. George Herbert's Lyrics. Baltimore: Johns Hopkins Press, 1968.

The Baptist Hymnal. Philadelphia: The American Baptist Publication Society, 1920.

The Church Hymnal. Boston: The Episcopal Parish Choir, 1894.

The Church Hymnary: A Collection of Hymns and Tunes for Public Worship. Compiler, Edwin Bedell. New York: Maynard, Merrill and Co. 1893.

The Clarendon Hymn Book. London: Oxford University Press, 1936.

The English Hymnal. London: Oxford University Press, 1933.

The English Psalter, Old Version. London: John Day, 1561.

The Evangelical Lutheran Hymn Book, St. Louis, Missouri: Concordia Publishing House, 1927.

The Hymnal of the Protestant Episcopal Church in the United States of America. New York: Church Pension Fund, 1940.

The New Encyclopedia Britannica. 10, 15th ed. London: Helen H. Benton, 1974.

The Oxford History of Music. III: The Music of the Seventeenth Century. New York: Cooper Square Publishers Inc., 1973.

The Oxford Hymn Book. Oxford: Clarendon Press, 1906.

The Psalms of David in Meeter. London. 1650.

Thomas, Nancy W. "The Philosophy of the Hymn." Papers of the Hymn Society of America, no. 21. 1956.

Vaughan, Henry, "Silurist", Sacred Poems and Pious Ejaculations. Ed. H. F. Lyte, London: George Bell and Sons, 1890.

Walton, Izaac. Walton's Lives. C. H. Dick ed. London; n.d. p. 57.

Walzer, Michael. The Revolution of the Saints: A Study in the Beginnings of Radical Politics. Cambridge: Harvard University Press, 1965.

Washburn, Charles C. Hymn Interpretations. Nashville, Cokesbury Press, 1938.

Watts, Isaac. <u>The Psalms, Hymns and Spiritual Songs of
    Isaac Watts, D.D.</u> Cincinati: Corey and Webster, 1836.

Wedgewood, Cicely V. <u>Poetry and Politics Under the Stuarts.</u>
    Cambridge: Cambridge University Press, 1960.

Willey, Basil. <u>The Seventeenth Century Background:
    Studies in the Thought of an Age in Relation to Poetry and
    Religion.</u> London: Chatto and Windus, 1942.

Whitemarsh, Caroline Snowden and Anne Guild. Compilers.
    <u>Hymns of the Ages: First Series.</u> Boston: James Osgood
    and Co., 1877.

Wither, George, <u>Hymnes and Songs of the Church.</u> New York:
    Burt Franklin Research, 1967. (Reprint of 1629 ed.)

_____. <u>The Scholar's Purgatory.</u> London: 1624.

INDEX

Lord Herbert of Cherbury, 112
Lowell, James Russell, 134
loyalty, 44, 129
Luther, Martin, 48
lyric, religion, 198
Macbeth, 169
man's insufficiency, 29
mariner's compass, 184
Marlowe, Christopher, 169
Mary Queen of Scots, 35
materialism, 186
medicine, as an art, 168
medieval times, relics of, 162, 184
medieval worship, 15
metaphor in hymns, 83, 85, 120, 162, 182
metaphysical conceit, 23
metaphysical concepts in hymns, 129, 164, 165
metaphysical poet, 119
metrical psalms, 46, 106
Middle Ages, 50
militaristic traditions in hymns, 132
Mexican Bay, 136
millenarianism, 143
Milton, John, 20, 44, 75, 115, 118, 142
missionaries, 177
More, Henry, 112
mutability in hymns, 160
mythology, 171, 184

National Anthem, Britain, 104
nationalistic hymns, 175, 195
Neale, John Mason, 87, 130
neoplatonism, 163, 172, 188n
Newman, Cardinal John Henry, 25, 78, 194
Newton, John, 25, 66
Newton, Sir Isaac, 159, 184
Non-conformist, 12
Non-Juror, 13

Oath of Allegiance, 146
Olney hymns, 25
orbital laws, 157
orginal sin, 56, 61

pagan belief, 184
pagan thought, 169, 171
papal power, 117
Parliamentarians, 98
Parliamentary Ecclesiastical Commission, 83
partisan age, 44, 112, 129

Clausius, Claudia

THE GENTLEMAN IS A TRAMP
Charlie Chaplin's Comedy

New York, Bern, Frankfurt/M., Paris, 1988, XII, 194 pp.
ISBN 0-8204-0459-4   hardback US $ 38.50/sFr. 57.50

Recommended prices – alterations reserved

Speaking to us in the language of comedy, Charlie Chaplin's art has always brought the world closer together. At the same time, however, it deliberately, often insidiously puts us at odds with ourselves. What is responsible for this comic tension? And why do we find the humour irresistibly attractive? The answer greets us with a polite bow and tip of the derby – the Tramp. But whose creation is this gentleman tramp? Who holds the strings of the film marionette, Charlie – the puppeteer or the audience? The answer is, of course, both. In the collaboration between Chaplin and the spectator a comedy ignites which challenges as it delights and pricks as it tickles.

Written in a straightforward manner with an eye to the amateur film enthusiast as well as the academic critic, this book investigates the Tramp character's evolution from the early shorts, through the sentimental middle period, to the darker, more cynical films and demonstrates how the comedy consistently uses the basic emotional/intellectual collision between Chaplin, the director, and Charlie, the Tramp, to evoke both laughter and reflection. Tackling both traditional and contemporary cinema criticism before analysing several of the key films The Gentleman is a Tramp takes a close-up look at the man in front of and behind the camera.

Contents: The Gentleman is a Tramp: Charlie Chaplin's Comedy explores the Chaplin/Charlie dichotomy in: 1) the dual function of the humour; 2) the duality of the comic medium; 3) the satire and parody of Chaplin's early work; 4) the montage technique of his middle period; 5) and the ironic process of his later works.
"A young mind applied to the work of an old master – the result is refreshingly new!" (Josef Skvorecky)

PETER LANG PUBLISHING, INC.
62 West 45th Street
USA – New York, NY 10036

Gill, Glenda E.

WHITE GREASE PAINT ON BLACK PERFORMERS
A Study of the Federal Theatre, 1935–1939

New York, Bern, Frankfurt/M., Paris, 1988. XVI, 220 pp.
American University Studies: Series 9, History. Vol. 40
ISBN 0-8204-0682-1   hardback US $ 36.00/sFr. 50.40

Recommended prices – alterations reserved

This theatre history work is an appraisal of the artistic and political impact of the Federal Theatre of The Great Depression on the careers of representative black actors. These include Canada Lee, Rex Ingram and Dooley Wilson. As an icebreaker, the Federal Theatre made it possible for black actors and audiences to enjoy benefits unknown previously: union protection, a theatre for the masses, a reduction of the stereotype, visibility that led to Broadway and to Hollywood, and an ensemble spirit. In spite of the tragedies of the WPA Project, there were significant triumphs. Contents: This book on theatre history is an appraisal of the artistic and political impact of the Federal Theatre of 1935–1939 on the careers of representative black actors. Rich in personal interviews, correspondence and rare archival finds.
". . . a remarkable account of the struggles of Black theater talents in the Federal Theater Project of the 1930s. Gill has retrieved the lives of giants whose talents had once flashed like comets across the American stage, but whose brilliance has been obscured by racial politics. This is a vital book for understanding Black Theater history." (James V. Hatch, Archives of Black American Cultural History)
"Glenda Gill tells the vivid, moving, sometimes tragic story of black actors in the Depression-era Federal Theatre Project. Through interviews and extensive research in documents still in private hands, she has uncovered valuable information otherwise inaccessible. This book fills in a missing chapter from the history of theatre in America. It makes an important contribution to black history, but like all great drama, it also brings out the broad significance from the detailed narrative of individual lives." (Donald G. Marshall, The University of Iowa)
"I have read this book with great pleasure . . . it covers some important figures at a very important time in the American theatre. Needless to say, it means a lot to me personally since, as the first co-director with Rose McClendon of the Negro theatre Unit of the Federal Theatre, I was directly involved in all but one of these lives . . . during those wonderfully exiting and formative days." (John Houseman)

PETER LANG PUBLISHING, INC.
62 West 45th Street
USA – New York, NY 10036

DATE DUE

HIGHSMITH   # 45220